Virtual Realms: Exploring the Boundless Frontiers of Immersive Experiences

Welcome to a world where reality meets imagination, where the limits of the physical realm dissolve, and where we embark on extraordinary journeys within the realms of virtual reality. In this book, we delve into the captivating realm of virtual reality (VR), a groundbreaking technology that has revolutionized the way we experience and interact with digital content.

Virtual reality has emerged as a transformative force, transporting us to breathtaking landscapes, ancient civilizations, futuristic cities, and even the depths of our own minds. It offers an unparalleled level of immersion and presence, enabling us to engage with digital worlds in ways we could only dream of before.

In this book, we embark on a comprehensive exploration of the boundless frontiers of virtual reality. We will unravel the underlying technology that powers VR, examine its historical roots, and dive into the diverse applications and industries it has revolutionized. From gaming and entertainment to education, healthcare, architecture, and beyond, we will witness how VR is reshaping our lives, industries, and perceptions.

Together, we will unravel the technical intricacies that make virtual reality possible, examining the hardware, software, and platforms that bring virtual experiences to life. We will delve into the art of world creation, exploring the techniques and principles behind designing immersive virtual environments. Additionally, we will delve into the social, cultural, and ethical implications of virtual reality, examining its impact on society, relationships, and human experiences.

As we navigate through this book, we invite you to open your mind to the possibilities that lie within virtual realms. Whether you are a curious explorer, an industry professional, or an enthusiast, this book will serve as your guide through the captivating landscapes and immersive experiences that virtual reality has to offer.

Join us as we embark on an extraordinary journey into Virtual Realms, where the power of technology and imagination collide, and where the frontiers of human experiences are redefined.

I. Introduction

- Definition and concept of virtual reality
- Historical background and evolution of virtual reality
- Significance and potential impact of virtual reality

II. Understanding Virtual Reality Technology

- Immersive experiences and sensory stimulation
- Hardware components: Headsets, controllers, and tracking systems
- Virtual reality content creation and development tools
- Advancements in virtual reality technology

III. Applications of Virtual Reality

- Gaming and entertainment
- Training and simulation
- Education and virtual classrooms
- Healthcare and therapy
- Architecture and design
- Travel and tourism
- Social interaction and communication

IV. Virtual Reality and the Human Experience

- Psychological and cognitive effects of virtual reality
- Presence and immersion in virtual environments
- Ethical considerations and user well-being
- Addressing motion sickness and discomfort

V. Industry Spotlight: Virtual Reality in Various Fields

- Virtual reality in the gaming industry
- Virtual reality in healthcare and medicine
- Virtual reality in education and training
- Virtual reality in architecture and design
- Virtual reality in the entertainment industry
- Virtual reality in marketing and advertising

VI. Virtual Reality Content Creation and Design

- 3D modeling and animation for virtual environments
- Interactive storytelling in virtual reality
- User interface and user experience design in virtual reality
- Sound design and spatial audio in virtual reality

VII. Challenges and Considerations in Virtual Reality

- Hardware limitations and affordability
- User comfort and health considerations
- Content accessibility and inclusivity
- Ethical and privacy concerns
- Legal and regulatory challenges

VIII. Virtual Reality and the Future

- Emerging trends and technologies in virtual reality
- Virtual reality in augmented reality ecosystems
- Virtual reality and artificial intelligence
- Predictions for the future of virtual reality

IX. Conclusion

- Recap of key concepts and insights
- Inspiring readers to embrace virtual reality
- Final thoughts on the transformative power of virtual reality

Definition and concept of virtual reality

Virtual reality (VR) is a technology that creates a simulated and immersive digital environment that users can interact with and explore. It aims to replicate real-world sensory experiences, such as sight, sound, and touch, in a virtual setting, giving users a sense of presence and immersion in a computer-generated world.

At its core, virtual reality is about creating a sense of "presence" or the feeling of being physically present in a different place or reality. Through the use of specialized hardware, such as head-mounted displays (HMDs), motion tracking sensors, and input devices, VR transports users to artificial environments that can be entirely fictional or based on real-world locations. By surrounding users with visuals and audio that respond to their movements and actions, VR aims to create a seamless and convincing illusion of being inside a virtual space.

Virtual reality can provide a wide range of experiences, from interactive games and simulations to educational and training applications, architectural visualizations, virtual tours, and even therapeutic interventions. The technology holds immense potential to revolutionize industries and fields such as gaming, entertainment, healthcare, education, architecture, engineering, and more.

In the realm of virtual reality, users have the freedom to explore and interact with digital objects, navigate virtual landscapes, manipulate virtual elements, and engage with other users in shared virtual spaces. The immersive nature of VR enables a level of engagement and interactivity that traditional media forms cannot replicate, fostering new possibilities for storytelling, collaboration, and creativity.

As virtual reality continues to evolve and improve, it holds the promise of transforming how we experience digital content, breaking down physical barriers, and opening up new avenues for communication, exploration, and self-expression. With its ability to transport us to worlds beyond our imagination, virtual reality is reshaping the way we perceive and interact with digital information, offering us a glimpse into the boundless possibilities of the virtual realm.

Historical background and evolution of virtual reality

The concept of virtual reality has its roots in the early 20th century, with the emergence of technology and ideas that paved the way for immersive experiences. The journey of virtual reality can be traced back to the stereoscope, invented in the 1830s, which provided users with a sense of depth perception by merging two flat images into a single 3D image. This early precursor set the foundation for the immersive experiences that virtual reality would later offer.

In the mid-20th century, scientists and inventors began envisioning more advanced forms of virtual reality. Ivan Sutherland, often referred to as the "Father of Computer Graphics," developed the "Sword of Damocles" in 1968, which is considered the first head-mounted display (HMD). This device, although primitive by today's standards, laid the groundwork for the immersive visual experiences that VR would later offer.

In the following decades, researchers and innovators continued to push the boundaries of virtual reality. The 1980s witnessed the development of early VR systems, such as the "DataGlove" and the "Virtual Reality Goggles," which allowed users to interact with virtual environments through hand movements and head tracking. However, the high costs and limited computing power of the time hindered widespread adoption.

The 1990s marked a significant era for virtual reality, with the introduction of more accessible and consumer-friendly VR devices. The release of the Sega VR headset and the Virtual Boy by

Nintendo brought VR experiences into the mainstream. However, technological limitations and issues, such as motion sickness, restricted the success and adoption of these early consumer VR products.

In the early 21st century, virtual reality made a resurgence with advancements in computing power, graphics capabilities, and motion tracking. The development of more sophisticated HMDs, such as the Oculus Rift, HTC Vive, and PlayStation VR, revolutionized the VR landscape. These devices offered higher resolution displays, improved tracking systems, and enhanced user experiences, fueling interest and excitement around virtual reality.

Alongside the hardware advancements, the growth of VR content and applications expanded the possibilities of virtual reality. VR experiences ranging from gaming and entertainment to education, training, and virtual tourism emerged, showcasing the versatility and potential of the technology.

Today, virtual reality continues to evolve rapidly, with ongoing advancements in hardware, software, and content creation. The introduction of standalone VR headsets, advancements in haptic feedback, and the integration of artificial intelligence and social interaction have further enriched the virtual reality experience.

As virtual reality technology becomes more accessible, affordable, and refined, it has the potential to revolutionize various industries, transform communication and entertainment, and provide new avenues for creativity, learning, and exploration. The historical journey of virtual reality has laid the foundation for a future where immersive digital experiences are seamlessly integrated into our daily lives.

Significance and potential impact of virtual reality

Virtual reality holds immense significance and has the potential to have a transformative impact on various aspects of our lives. By creating immersive and interactive digital environments that simulate real or imagined worlds, virtual reality has the power to revolutionize how we experience, interact with, and perceive the world around us.

One of the key areas where virtual reality is making waves is in entertainment and gaming. With VR headsets and systems, users can step into virtual worlds and become active participants in their favorite games, movies, or virtual experiences. The level of immersion and engagement offered by virtual reality enhances storytelling, delivers new levels of realism, and creates unforgettable experiences. Virtual reality has the potential to redefine entertainment and revolutionize the way we consume media.

In addition to entertainment, virtual reality has profound implications for education and training. It allows learners to engage in realistic and interactive simulations that enhance their understanding and retention of complex concepts. Fields such as medicine, engineering, and aviation benefit from VR-based training programs that provide hands-on experiences without real-world risks. Virtual reality has the potential to democratize education and make learning more accessible and engaging for people around the world.

Virtual reality also has the power to redefine social interaction and communication. With VR headsets, people can connect with each other in shared virtual spaces, even when physically separated by great distances. Virtual reality enables immersive teleconferencing, virtual meetings, and collaborative workspaces, fostering a sense of presence and enhancing remote collaboration. It opens up new possibilities for socializing, creating communities, and experiencing events together in virtual environments.

Moreover, virtual reality has the potential to transform industries such as architecture, design, and real estate by offering immersive 3D visualizations of spaces and environments. It enables professionals to explore and interact with virtual representations of their projects, improving design processes, reducing costs, and enhancing decision-making.

Beyond these areas, virtual reality holds promise in healthcare, therapy, rehabilitation, and the exploration of new frontiers in scientific research. It can be used to treat phobias, alleviate pain, and provide therapeutic experiences. Virtual reality also enables us to visit places we may never physically reach, such as outer space or ancient historical sites, and provides a platform for scientific exploration and discovery.

The potential impact of virtual reality extends beyond individual domains and has the power to reshape how we experience and interact with the world. As technology continues to evolve, virtual reality has the potential to bridge the gap between physical and digital realms, blurring the boundaries and unlocking infinite possibilities for creativity, innovation, and human connection.

Immersive experiences and sensory stimulation

One of the most captivating aspects of virtual reality is its ability to provide immersive experiences and stimulate our senses in ways that traditional media cannot. Through the use of VR headsets and motion-tracking devices, virtual reality creates a sensory-rich environment that engages our sight, hearing, and even touch, transporting us to entirely new realms and experiences.

Visual immersion is a key component of virtual reality. VR headsets, equipped with high-resolution displays and wide field-of-view, wrap around our field of vision, blocking out the real world and replacing it with a digital landscape. This visual immersion gives us a sense of presence and allows us to feel like we are truly inside the virtual world. Whether it's exploring a fantastical realm, diving deep into the ocean, or standing on the surface of a distant planet, virtual reality can transport us to places we could only dream of.

In addition to visual immersion, virtual reality incorporates spatial audio technology to enhance the auditory experience. By simulating realistic 3D soundscapes, virtual reality can create a sense of depth and directionality, making the virtual environment feel more lifelike. Sound cues and effects further enhance the sense of presence and immersion, adding to the overall realism of the virtual experience.

Moreover, some advanced virtual reality systems incorporate haptic feedback technology, allowing users to feel physical sensations within the virtual world. This can range from subtle vibrations or pressure feedback to more intricate haptic suits that provide a full-body tactile experience. By engaging our sense of touch, virtual reality adds another layer of immersion, enabling us to interact with virtual objects, feel textures, and even experience the sensation of being touched by virtual characters or objects.

The combination of visual, auditory, and haptic stimulation creates a truly immersive experience that can transport us to different times, places, and realities. It enables us to explore and interact with virtual worlds as if they were real, unlocking new dimensions of storytelling, gaming, education, and more. The immersive nature of virtual reality has the power to evoke emotions, trigger memories, and leave a lasting impact on our senses, making it a powerful medium for entertainment, learning, and creativity.

As virtual reality technology continues to advance, with improvements in display resolution, audio quality, and haptic feedback, the potential for even more immersive experiences grows. The ability to stimulate our senses in such a profound way opens up endless possibilities for virtual reality to revolutionize industries, transform the way we experience media, and provide unparalleled opportunities for exploration, entertainment, and self-expression.

Hardware components: Headsets, controllers, and tracking systems

Virtual reality experiences are made possible through a combination of hardware components that work together to create an immersive and interactive environment. These components include headsets, controllers, and tracking systems, each playing a crucial role in the overall virtual reality experience.

1. Headsets: At the heart of virtual reality is the headset, which is worn over the eyes and serves as the primary interface between the user and the virtual world. VR headsets are equipped with high-resolution displays, typically OLED or LCD screens, that deliver crisp and detailed visuals to the user's eyes. They are designed to provide a wide field of view, mimicking the natural human vision and creating a sense of immersion. Some popular VR headset models include Oculus Rift, HTC Vive, and PlayStation VR.

2. Controllers: To interact with the virtual environment, users rely on controllers. These handheld devices are equipped with buttons, triggers, joysticks, and touch-sensitive surfaces that allow users to manipulate virtual objects, navigate menus, and perform actions within the virtual world. Controllers come in various forms, ranging from handheld gamepad-style controllers to motion-tracked controllers that can detect the user's hand movements and gestures. These controllers enhance the sense of presence and enable intuitive interaction with the virtual environment.

3. Tracking Systems: Tracking systems are responsible for accurately capturing the user's movements and translating them into the virtual world. They ensure that the user's position and orientation are tracked in real-time, allowing for precise and responsive interactions. There are different types of tracking systems, including inside-out tracking and outside-in tracking. Inside-out tracking uses sensors on the headset or controllers to track their position in relation to the user's surroundings, while outside-in tracking involves external sensors or cameras placed in the room to track the user's movements. These tracking systems enable users to freely explore and interact with the virtual environment, providing a seamless and immersive experience.

Additionally, some advanced virtual reality setups may include other peripherals and accessories such as haptic feedback devices, motion platforms, and eye-tracking systems. These components further enhance the realism and immersion of the virtual experience, adding tactile sensations, dynamic movements, and even gaze-based interactions.

The continuous advancements in virtual reality hardware contribute to improved comfort, higher fidelity visuals, more accurate tracking, and enhanced user interaction. As technology progresses, we can expect to see lighter, more ergonomic headsets, more intuitive and versatile controllers, and increasingly sophisticated tracking systems, all working together to deliver ever more immersive and engaging virtual reality experiences.

Virtual reality content creation and development tools

Creating virtual reality content requires specialized tools and software that enable developers to design, build, and optimize immersive experiences. These tools empower content creators to bring their ideas to life and deliver engaging virtual reality environments. Here are some essential virtual reality content creation and development tools:

1. 3D Modeling Software: 3D modeling software, such as Blender, Autodesk Maya, or ZBrush, is used to create and design virtual objects, characters, environments, and props. These tools allow developers to sculpt, texture, and animate 3D assets with precision, ensuring realistic and visually appealing virtual worlds.

2. Game Engines: Game engines serve as the backbone for virtual reality content development. Popular game engines like Unity and Unreal Engine provide a wide range of features and functionalities, including rendering, physics simulation, scripting, and asset management. These engines offer VR-specific toolkits and frameworks, simplifying the process of building interactive and immersive VR experiences.

3. Virtual Reality SDKs: Software Development Kits (SDKs) specific to virtual reality, such as Oculus SDK, SteamVR SDK, or Google VR SDK, provide developers with the necessary APIs, libraries, and tools to integrate VR capabilities into their applications. These SDKs handle tasks such as head tracking, input handling, and

rendering optimizations, enabling developers to create VR experiences that run smoothly and efficiently.

4. Audio Tools: Sound plays a crucial role in creating immersive virtual reality experiences. Audio tools like FMOD Studio or Wwise allow developers to design and implement spatial audio, creating realistic and dynamic soundscapes that enhance the sense of presence in the virtual world.

5. VR Prototyping and Design Tools: Prototyping and design tools like Sketchbox, Gravity Sketch, or Tilt Brush enable creators to rapidly iterate and visualize their VR concepts. These tools often leverage motion controllers and allow designers to sketch, sculpt, or create 3D prototypes in a virtual space, facilitating the exploration of ideas and the development of immersive VR environments.

6. Performance Optimization Tools: Optimizing performance is essential to ensure a smooth and comfortable VR experience. Tools like NVIDIA Nsight, Intel GPA, or Unity Profiler help developers analyze and optimize their VR applications, identifying performance bottlenecks, reducing latency, and maximizing frame rates for a seamless VR experience.

7. Collaboration Platforms: Virtual reality collaboration platforms, such as Mozilla Hubs or Spatial, provide tools for remote teams to work together in virtual environments. These platforms enable real-time collaboration, allowing developers, designers, and stakeholders to meet, discuss, and review VR projects in a shared virtual space.

By leveraging these content creation and development tools, developers and creators can unleash their creativity and build compelling virtual reality experiences. As technology continues to advance, we can expect more innovative tools and software to emerge, further empowering the VR community and pushing the boundaries of immersive content creation.

Advancements in virtual reality technology

Virtual reality technology has witnessed significant advancements in recent years, driving the evolution and widespread adoption of immersive experiences. These advancements have revolutionized the capabilities of virtual reality, enhancing its realism, comfort, and accessibility. Here are some notable advancements in virtual reality technology:

1. Higher Resolution Displays: Virtual reality headsets now feature high-resolution displays with improved pixel density. This allows for sharper and more detailed visuals, reducing the screen-door effect and enhancing the overall visual fidelity of the virtual environment.

2. Wireless and Standalone Headsets: Early virtual reality systems relied on wired connections to a computer, limiting user mobility. However, the development of wireless and standalone headsets, such as the Oculus Quest series and the HTC Vive Focus, has freed users from cables, providing a more convenient and immersive VR experience.

3. Inside-Out Tracking: Traditionally, virtual reality systems required external sensors or base stations to track the user's movements. Inside-out tracking eliminates the need for external sensors by integrating cameras and sensors directly into the VR headset. This technology enables more natural and unrestricted movement in virtual environments.

4. Improved Controllers and Haptic Feedback: Virtual reality controllers have undergone significant improvements, offering more precise tracking and

enhanced haptic feedback. These advancements allow users to interact with virtual objects and environments in a more intuitive and realistic manner, further enhancing immersion.

5. Eye Tracking: Eye-tracking technology has been integrated into some virtual reality headsets, enabling more sophisticated interactions and enhanced user experiences. Eye tracking allows for foveated rendering, where the highest level of detail is displayed only in the area the user is directly looking at, optimizing performance and reducing the rendering load on the system.

6. Realistic Audio and Spatial Sound: Virtual reality audio has evolved to deliver more immersive and realistic soundscapes. Spatial audio techniques simulate sound propagation and three-dimensional audio cues, enhancing the sense of presence and immersiveness within the virtual environment.

7. Augmented Reality Overlays: Augmented reality (AR) overlays in virtual reality experiences blend virtual content with the real world, creating mixed reality experiences. This technology enables users to see and interact with virtual objects or data within their physical environment, opening up new possibilities for productivity, gaming, and information visualization.

8. Social and Multiplayer Experiences: Virtual reality platforms now offer robust social and multiplayer features, allowing users to connect and interact with others in shared virtual spaces. These advancements in social VR technology enable collaborative experiences, virtual meetings, and social gatherings, fostering a sense of presence and community in the virtual world.

As virtual reality technology continues to evolve, we can expect further advancements in areas such as hand tracking, facial expression tracking, haptic suits, and improved locomotion solutions. These advancements will continue to push the boundaries of what is possible in virtual reality, creating even more immersive, engaging, and realistic experiences.

Gaming and entertainment

Gaming and entertainment have been at the forefront of virtual reality (VR) since its inception, and they continue to be major driving forces behind its popularity and adoption. VR gaming provides players with an unprecedented level of immersion, allowing them to step into virtual worlds and interact with them in ways that were previously unimaginable. Here are some key aspects of gaming and entertainment in the realm of virtual reality:

1. Immersive Gameplay: Virtual reality gaming offers a level of immersion that traditional gaming cannot match. With VR headsets and motion controllers, players can physically engage in the game world, moving their bodies, interacting with objects, and engaging in realistic gameplay mechanics. This creates a heightened sense of presence and agency, making the gaming experience more engaging and captivating.

2. Virtual Worlds and Environments: Virtual reality opens up a whole new realm of possibilities for game developers to create expansive and visually stunning virtual worlds. Players can explore fantastical landscapes, visit iconic locations, and interact with dynamic environments in ways that blur the line between the real and virtual worlds.

3. Multiplayer and Social Experiences: Virtual reality facilitates social interactions and multiplayer experiences on a whole new level. Players can meet up with friends in virtual spaces, join multiplayer games, and communicate through voice chat or even full-

body avatars. This fosters a sense of community and connection among players, transcending geographical boundaries.

4. Enhanced Immersion with Haptic Feedback: Haptic feedback devices, such as haptic vests or gloves, add a tactile dimension to virtual reality gaming. They provide physical sensations and vibrations that correspond to in-game events, enhancing the sense of immersion and making gameplay more realistic and engaging.

5. New Gameplay Mechanics: Virtual reality introduces new gameplay mechanics that leverage the technology's unique capabilities. For example, players can physically duck behind cover, lean around corners, or use hand gestures to interact with objects in the virtual environment. These intuitive and natural interactions enhance gameplay and create novel experiences.

6. Virtual Reality Arcades and Experiences: The rise of virtual reality has led to the emergence of dedicated VR arcades and entertainment venues. These spaces offer the opportunity for people to experience high-end VR technology and play a variety of VR games and experiences without needing to own their own equipment. It provides a social and accessible way for people to explore the immersive world of VR.

7. Cinematic and Interactive Storytelling: Virtual reality has opened up new avenues for cinematic experiences and interactive storytelling. VR films and interactive narratives allow viewers to be fully immersed in the story, exploring different perspectives and influencing the outcome of the narrative. This blurs the line between traditional passive viewing and active participation.

Virtual reality has revolutionized gaming and entertainment by offering unparalleled immersion, interactivity, and the ability to transport users to new worlds. It continues to push the boundaries of what is possible in gaming, storytelling, and social experiences. As technology advances and VR becomes more accessible, we can expect even more innovative and groundbreaking experiences in the world of gaming and entertainment.

Training and simulation

Training and simulation are key applications of virtual reality (VR) that have revolutionized various industries. VR provides a safe and immersive environment for individuals to acquire new skills, practice real-life scenarios, and engage in experiential learning. Here's an overview of the significance and benefits of training and simulation in virtual reality:

1. Realistic and Immersive Training: Virtual reality allows trainees to engage in realistic simulations that closely mimic real-world environments and scenarios. From medical procedures to military operations, VR training offers a safe and controlled space where individuals can practice without the risk or cost associated with traditional training methods. This immersive experience enables trainees to develop practical skills, muscle memory, and decision-making abilities in a highly realistic setting.

2. Enhanced Engagement and Retention: The immersive nature of VR training fosters higher levels of engagement and active participation. Trainees are more likely to be fully focused and invested in the training experience, leading to better retention of information and skills. The ability to interact with virtual objects and receive immediate feedback also enhances the learning process, allowing trainees to correct mistakes and refine their techniques in real-time.

3. Cost and Resource Efficiency: VR training can significantly reduce costs associated with traditional training methods. It eliminates the need for expensive

equipment, physical spaces, and materials required for hands-on training. With VR, training programs can be conducted remotely, saving time and travel expenses. Additionally, simulations can be easily modified and repeated, allowing for efficient use of resources and scalability in training programs.

4. Risk-Free Environment: Virtual reality provides a safe and controlled environment for training in high-risk industries or scenarios. It allows trainees to learn from mistakes without any real-world consequences. For example, surgeons can practice complex procedures, pilots can train in flight simulations, and emergency responders can prepare for crisis situations, all without jeopardizing lives or assets. This risk-free environment encourages experimentation, problem-solving, and skill development.

5. Customization and Adaptability: VR training can be tailored to specific needs and requirements. Training scenarios can be adjusted based on skill levels, learning objectives, or individual preferences. The ability to simulate different scenarios and variables allows trainees to experience a wide range of situations, preparing them for real-life challenges. Additionally, VR training can be easily updated and upgraded as new knowledge and techniques emerge, ensuring that training programs remain relevant and up-to-date.

6. Cross-Industry Applications: VR training extends beyond traditional sectors such as healthcare and defense. It has found applications in industries such as manufacturing, construction, automotive, hospitality, and more. From assembly line operations to customer service interactions, VR simulations provide hands-on experience and enable trainees to develop skills applicable to their specific roles.

7. Performance Assessment and Analytics: Virtual reality training platforms often incorporate performance

assessment and analytics tools. These tools provide valuable data on trainees' progress, performance metrics, and areas for improvement. Trainers and organizations can track trainees' development, identify strengths and weaknesses, and provide targeted feedback to enhance learning outcomes.

Virtual reality training and simulation have the potential to revolutionize education and professional development. By leveraging the immersive and interactive capabilities of VR, individuals can acquire skills, enhance their knowledge, and gain confidence in a realistic and engaging environment. As technology continues to advance, the potential applications and benefits of VR training will only expand, driving innovation across industries and fostering a new era of experiential learning.

Education and virtual classrooms

Virtual reality (VR) has opened up new possibilities for education by creating immersive and engaging virtual classrooms. Virtual classrooms leverage the power of VR technology to provide students with unique learning experiences that go beyond traditional textbooks and lectures. Here's an overview of the significance and benefits of virtual classrooms in education:

1. Immersive Learning Environment: Virtual classrooms transport students to virtual worlds where they can interact with three-dimensional objects, explore simulations, and engage in realistic scenarios. This immersive environment enhances students' engagement and active participation in the learning process. They can manipulate objects, conduct experiments, and experience historical events firsthand, making learning more interactive and memorable.

2. Global Access and Inclusivity: Virtual classrooms break down geographical barriers and provide equal access to education. Students from different parts of the world can connect in the same virtual space, fostering cultural exchange and diverse perspectives. Virtual classrooms also enable individuals with physical disabilities or limitations to participate in educational activities that might be challenging in traditional settings, promoting inclusivity and equal opportunities.

3. Interactive Collaboration: Virtual classrooms facilitate collaborative learning experiences. Students can work together on projects, solve problems, and engage in

group discussions, just as they would in physical classrooms. The ability to communicate and collaborate in real-time within a shared virtual environment promotes teamwork, communication skills, and cooperation among students.

4. Personalized Learning: Virtual classrooms have the potential to adapt to individual learning styles and preferences. Educators can create personalized learning experiences by tailoring the content, pace, and level of difficulty to each student's needs. VR technology allows for customized feedback and assessments, enabling students to receive immediate guidance and support based on their performance.

5. Experiential and Practical Learning: Virtual classrooms provide opportunities for experiential and practical learning. Students can engage in virtual field trips, explore historical landmarks, or conduct virtual science experiments. These hands-on experiences foster a deeper understanding of concepts and encourage critical thinking skills. Virtual simulations also allow students to practice real-life scenarios, such as medical procedures or architectural designs, in a safe and controlled environment.

6. Engagement and Motivation: The immersive nature of virtual classrooms increases student engagement and motivation. The ability to visually and interactively explore educational content stimulates curiosity and makes learning more enjoyable. Virtual environments can be gamified, incorporating elements of competition, rewards, and challenges, which further motivates students to actively participate and excel in their studies.

7. Cost and Resource Efficiency: Virtual classrooms can be a cost-effective alternative to traditional educational methods. They eliminate the need for physical infrastructure, transportation expenses, and printed

materials. Educators can create and distribute digital resources, reducing costs and environmental impact. Virtual classrooms also enable scalability, allowing educational institutions to reach a larger number of students without constraints of physical space.

8. Continuous Learning and Professional Development: Virtual classrooms extend beyond K-12 education and are increasingly utilized in higher education and professional development. Virtual platforms offer online courses, workshops, and training programs, allowing individuals to enhance their skills and knowledge from anywhere in the world. Lifelong learners can access a wide range of educational opportunities, fostering continuous learning and career advancement.

Virtual classrooms have the potential to transform education by providing innovative and engaging learning experiences. As VR technology continues to evolve and become more accessible, the integration of virtual classrooms into educational systems will expand. This shift towards immersive and interactive learning environments holds great promise for enhancing student outcomes, fostering global collaboration, and revolutionizing the way knowledge is acquired and shared.

Healthcare and therapy

Virtual reality (VR) is revolutionizing the healthcare industry by offering new possibilities in patient care, medical training, and therapy. VR technology creates immersive and interactive virtual environments that have shown significant potential in various healthcare applications. Here's an overview of how VR is transforming healthcare and therapy:

1. Pain Management: Virtual reality has proven to be an effective tool in pain management, especially for patients undergoing painful medical procedures or experiencing chronic pain. By immersing patients in virtual environments that distract and engage their senses, VR can help reduce the perception of pain and discomfort. This can minimize the need for traditional pain medications and provide a non-invasive alternative for pain relief.

2. Medical Training and Simulation: VR enables realistic medical training simulations for healthcare professionals. Medical students and practitioners can practice complex procedures, surgical techniques, and emergency scenarios in virtual environments that mimic real-life situations. VR simulations provide a safe and controlled space for learning, allowing healthcare professionals to hone their skills, improve decision-making, and gain confidence before performing procedures on actual patients.

3. Mental Health Therapy: Virtual reality has shown promise in the field of mental health therapy. VR-based therapy can simulate anxiety-inducing situations,

phobias, and post-traumatic stress disorder (PTSD) scenarios, allowing patients to confront and manage their fears in a controlled environment. VR therapy can also create relaxing and soothing environments to promote stress reduction, mindfulness, and emotional well-being. This immersive approach to therapy can enhance treatment outcomes and provide a novel way to address mental health challenges.

4. Rehabilitation and Physical Therapy: Virtual reality is being used to support rehabilitation and physical therapy programs. By creating interactive and engaging virtual environments, patients can perform therapeutic exercises and activities in a more motivating and enjoyable manner. VR-based rehabilitation helps improve motor skills, balance, and coordination while providing real-time feedback and tracking progress. It also allows for remote monitoring and tele-rehabilitation, enabling patients to access therapy sessions from their homes.

5. Medical Visualization and Planning: Virtual reality enhances medical visualization by creating detailed and three-dimensional representations of anatomical structures, medical imaging data, and complex medical concepts. Surgeons can use VR to explore patient-specific anatomy before surgical procedures, improving surgical planning and reducing risks. VR also enables medical professionals to collaborate and communicate visually, enhancing interdisciplinary teamwork and patient education.

6. Empathy and Patient Experience: Virtual reality has the potential to foster empathy and enhance the patient experience. By immersing healthcare providers in simulated patient scenarios, VR can help them better understand and empathize with patients' perspectives, ultimately improving the quality of care. VR can also transport patients to virtual environments that

promote relaxation, positive emotions, and well-being, enhancing their overall healthcare experience.

7. Telemedicine and Remote Care: VR can facilitate remote healthcare services through telemedicine applications. Patients in remote locations or with limited mobility can access healthcare consultations, therapies, and monitoring through virtual platforms. VR-based telemedicine allows for real-time interactions with healthcare professionals, bridging geographical gaps and increasing access to quality care, especially in underserved areas.

The adoption of virtual reality in healthcare is driven by its potential to enhance patient outcomes, improve medical training, and increase accessibility to healthcare services. As VR technology continues to advance and become more affordable, it is expected to play an increasingly significant role in the healthcare industry, transforming the way healthcare is delivered, experienced, and accessed.

Architecture and design

In the realm of virtual reality (VR), architecture and design are undergoing a remarkable transformation. VR technology enables architects, designers, and clients to immerse themselves in virtual environments that simulate architectural spaces, offering new ways to visualize, analyze, and experience designs. Here's an exploration of how virtual reality is revolutionizing architecture and design:

1. Visualization and Spatial Understanding: VR allows architects and designers to visualize and experience their designs in a highly immersive and realistic manner. By donning a VR headset, stakeholders can walk through virtual buildings, interact with objects and materials, and get a sense of scale and proportion. This immersive experience provides a deeper understanding of spatial relationships, lighting conditions, and the overall feel of a design before it is built physically. It enables early-stage design exploration and facilitates more informed decision-making.

2. Design Iteration and Collaboration: VR enhances the design iteration process by providing a platform for rapid prototyping and experimentation. Architects and designers can quickly create and modify virtual models, exploring different design options and assessing their impact. VR also facilitates collaborative design reviews, enabling multiple stakeholders to simultaneously immerse themselves in the virtual space, offer feedback, and make decisions in real-time. This collaborative and

iterative workflow improves communication, reduces errors, and accelerates the design process.

3. Human-Centered Design and User Experience: VR empowers architects and designers to create human-centered designs by simulating the experience of users within virtual environments. By integrating user feedback and conducting virtual user testing, designers can evaluate factors such as ergonomics, accessibility, and the overall user experience. This approach helps refine designs to better meet the needs and preferences of end-users, resulting in more user-centric architectural and design solutions.

4. Conceptual Design and Storytelling: VR serves as a powerful tool for conveying design concepts and telling compelling design narratives. Architects and designers can use virtual reality to communicate their vision to clients, stakeholders, and the general public. By immersing viewers in virtual environments, designers can evoke emotional responses, highlight design features, and articulate the intended atmosphere and ambiance. This immersive storytelling capability enhances the engagement and understanding of design concepts, facilitating better appreciation and decision-making.

5. Sustainable Design and Analysis: VR aids in the analysis and evaluation of sustainable design strategies. Architects can simulate and analyze factors such as natural lighting, thermal performance, and energy consumption within virtual environments. This allows for the optimization of design solutions to achieve energy efficiency, comfort, and sustainability goals. VR also enables stakeholders to experience and understand the benefits of sustainable design features, fostering awareness and commitment to environmentally conscious architecture.

6. Cultural Preservation and Heritage Documentation:

Virtual reality plays a vital role in the preservation and documentation of cultural heritage sites and historical architecture. Through 3D scanning and modeling, virtual representations of endangered or inaccessible sites can be created. VR allows users to explore and interact with these virtual reconstructions, promoting cultural appreciation and conservation efforts. Additionally, VR-based experiences can recreate historical contexts, providing immersive educational opportunities to learn about architectural history and cultural heritage.

7. Virtual Design Collaboration and Remote Work: Virtual reality facilitates global collaboration in the architectural and design industries. Design teams located in different geographic locations can collaborate in real-time within shared virtual spaces. This allows for seamless communication, design coordination, and decision-making, reducing the need for travel and enabling remote work. VR-based collaboration platforms enhance efficiency, productivity, and inclusivity in the design process.

As virtual reality technology continues to advance, architecture and design professionals are embracing its potential to revolutionize the industry. VR offers a transformative toolset that enhances visualization, collaboration, user experience, sustainability analysis, cultural preservation, and global design collaboration. With its ability to create immersive and interactive virtual environments, virtual reality is reshaping the way architects and designers conceive, communicate, and realize their creative visions.

Travel and tourism

Virtual reality (VR) is reshaping the travel and tourism industry by offering immersive and transformative experiences to travelers. With VR, people can explore destinations, visit landmarks, and engage in virtual travel without leaving their homes. Here's an overview of how VR is revolutionizing travel and tourism:

1. Virtual Destination Exploration: VR enables users to virtually visit destinations around the world. Through 360-degree videos and immersive VR experiences, travelers can explore famous landmarks, natural wonders, and cultural sites as if they were physically present. Virtual destination exploration allows for virtual tourism, providing a taste of different locations and inspiring travelers to plan future trips.

2. Enhanced Travel Planning: VR assists travelers in making informed decisions during the travel planning process. By offering virtual tours of hotels, resorts, and vacation rentals, travelers can experience accommodations before booking. VR also enables users to visualize transportation options, such as virtual walkthroughs of airplanes, trains, or cruise ships, helping them choose the most suitable mode of travel. This enhanced visualization aids in selecting travel experiences that align with personal preferences and needs.

3. Immersive Cultural Experiences: VR brings cultural immersion to a new level by allowing travelers to experience local traditions, festivals, and customs

virtually. Through VR, users can participate in virtual cultural events, explore museums and art galleries, and engage in interactive experiences that showcase the heritage and traditions of a destination. This immersive cultural exposure enhances travelers' understanding and appreciation of diverse cultures.

4. Virtual Reality Sightseeing: VR offers the opportunity to virtually visit iconic landmarks and attractions. Travelers can experience virtual sightseeing tours, guided by local experts who provide insights and historical context. These virtual tours can be customized based on personal interests, allowing travelers to delve into specific aspects of a destination's history, architecture, or natural beauty.

5. Travel Training and Education: VR serves as a powerful educational tool for travelers. It can provide training simulations for adventure activities, language learning, and cultural etiquette. VR-based language learning programs allow users to practice their language skills in immersive virtual environments, preparing them for real-world interactions during their travels. This educational aspect of VR enhances travelers' preparedness and enriches their travel experiences.

6. Accessible Travel Experiences: VR has the potential to make travel accessible to individuals who face physical or mobility limitations. By offering virtual travel experiences, people with disabilities can explore destinations and engage in activities that may not be feasible in the physical world. VR-based accessibility initiatives promote inclusivity in the travel industry and allow everyone to experience the joy of travel.

7. Sustainable and Eco-Friendly Travel: VR contributes to sustainable travel practices by reducing the carbon footprint associated with long-distance travel. Through virtual travel experiences, individuals can satisfy their wanderlust without the need for extensive air travel,

thus minimizing environmental impact. Virtual reality serves as a complementary option for eco-conscious travelers who want to explore destinations in a more sustainable way.

8. Travel Inspiration and Marketing: VR acts as a powerful marketing tool for destinations, hotels, and travel agencies. By creating compelling and immersive virtual experiences, travel providers can inspire potential travelers and showcase the unique aspects of their offerings. Virtual reality travel content can be shared through social media, websites, and VR platforms, generating excitement and motivating travelers to explore new destinations.

Virtual reality is transforming the way people experience and engage with travel. Through virtual destination exploration, enhanced travel planning, cultural immersion, and educational experiences, VR opens up a world of possibilities for travelers. With its ability to provide immersive and interactive virtual travel experiences, VR is expanding the boundaries of travel and tourism, making it more accessible, sustainable, and enriching for travelers around the globe.

Social interaction and communication

Social interaction and communication are vital aspects of human connection, and virtual reality (VR) is revolutionizing these elements by providing immersive and interactive experiences. Here's an overview of how VR is transforming social interaction and communication:

1. Virtual Social Spaces: VR creates virtual environments where people can gather, socialize, and interact with each other in real-time. These virtual social spaces can be designed as virtual worlds, social VR platforms, or multiplayer VR games. Users can join these spaces using VR headsets and avatars, representing themselves in the virtual world. They can communicate through voice chat or text, engage in activities together, and build meaningful connections.

2. Avatars and Personalization: In VR, users can create personalized avatars that represent themselves in the virtual environment. Avatars can be customized to reflect personal preferences, appearance, and even gestures. This level of personalization allows individuals to express themselves in unique ways and enhances the sense of identity and presence in virtual social interactions.

3. Non-Verbal Communication: VR enables non-verbal communication cues that mimic real-life interactions. Through hand tracking, body movements, and gestures, users can convey emotions, express themselves, and engage in natural social interactions. These non-verbal cues enhance the sense of presence and authenticity,

making virtual social interactions more engaging and meaningful.

4. Virtual Meetings and Collaboration: VR facilitates virtual meetings and collaborative workspaces, enabling remote teams to come together and collaborate in a shared virtual environment. Users can hold virtual meetings, share presentations, and collaborate on projects in a more immersive and interactive manner. This enhances communication and teamwork, even when physically separated.

5. Live Events and Concerts: VR enables the experience of attending live events, concerts, and performances virtually. Users can participate in virtual concerts and watch live streams of events, providing a sense of presence and connection with performers and fellow audience members. This expands access to cultural and entertainment experiences, regardless of geographic location.

6. Social Games and Activities: VR offers a wide range of social games and activities that allow users to interact and engage with others in a virtual setting. Multiplayer VR games provide opportunities for cooperative or competitive gameplay, fostering social connections and shared experiences. Users can also participate in virtual sports, team-based challenges, and interactive experiences that promote social interaction and friendly competition.

7. Remote Socialization: VR breaks down geographical barriers and allows people to connect and socialize regardless of their physical location. Friends, family, and loved ones can come together in virtual environments, celebrate special occasions, and engage in activities as if they were physically present. VR provides a sense of togetherness and closeness, even when separated by distance.

8. Cross-Cultural Interactions: VR facilitates cross-cultural

interactions and the exploration of diverse perspectives. Users can connect with individuals from different countries and cultures, fostering global understanding and empathy. Virtual travel experiences, language exchanges, and cultural events enable users to learn from and engage with people from around the world, expanding their horizons and promoting intercultural dialogue.

Virtual reality is revolutionizing social interaction and communication by creating immersive and engaging environments where people can connect, collaborate, and experience shared moments. Through virtual social spaces, personalized avatars, non-verbal communication, virtual meetings, live events, social games, and cross-cultural interactions, VR is redefining how we connect and build relationships. As VR technology continues to advance, the potential for transformative social experiences will only grow, opening up new possibilities for human connection in the digital realm.

Psychological and cognitive effects of virtual reality

Virtual reality (VR) has the potential to impact our psychological and cognitive processes in various ways. Here are some key effects of virtual reality on the human mind:

1. Presence and Immersion: VR can create a strong sense of presence and immersion, where users feel like they are truly present in the virtual environment. This heightened sense of presence can evoke emotional responses and a feeling of "being there," leading to a more immersive and engaging experience.

2. Emotional Responses: VR experiences can elicit strong emotional reactions. By placing users in immersive environments, VR can evoke emotions such as joy, fear, excitement, and empathy. This emotional engagement can enhance the overall impact of virtual experiences and make them more memorable.

3. Cognitive Load and Information Processing: VR can impose a significant cognitive load on users. The complexity of virtual environments, the need to process visual and auditory stimuli, and the requirement to perform tasks or make decisions in real-time can challenge cognitive resources. This can result in increased mental effort, attentional demands, and information processing.

4. Spatial Cognition and Navigation: Virtual environments often require users to navigate and interact with 3D spaces. Through spatial mapping and realistic

representations, VR can enhance spatial cognition and improve spatial awareness and navigation skills. Users can develop a better understanding of spatial relationships and mental maps within the virtual environment.

5. Learning and Skill Acquisition: VR has shown promise as a powerful tool for learning and skill acquisition. By simulating real-world scenarios, VR can provide hands-on training experiences in a safe and controlled environment. This can be particularly effective for skill development in fields such as medicine, aviation, engineering, and military training.

6. Rehabilitation and Therapy: Virtual reality has been used in therapeutic contexts to aid in physical and psychological rehabilitation. By creating virtual scenarios that mimic real-life situations, VR can assist in exposure therapy, pain management, and motor skill rehabilitation. It can also be used for relaxation and stress reduction through immersive and calming experiences.

7. Memory and Recall: VR experiences can have an impact on memory and recall. The vivid and immersive nature of virtual environments can enhance memory encoding and retrieval, making virtual experiences more memorable than traditional forms of media. This can be leveraged in educational settings and training programs to improve retention and recall of information.

8. Empathy and Perspective-Taking: VR has the potential to foster empathy and perspective-taking by allowing users to embody different characters or experience different situations. Through immersive storytelling and interactive narratives, VR can create a sense of presence and emotional connection, leading to increased empathy and understanding of others' experiences.

It's important to note that the psychological and cognitive effects of virtual reality can vary from person to person and depend on factors such as individual susceptibility, the nature of the VR experience, and the specific context in which it is used. Ethical considerations, including the potential for negative effects or misuse, should also be taken into account when designing and deploying VR experiences.

Presence and immersion in virtual environments

Presence and immersion are key concepts in the field of virtual reality (VR) that describe the degree to which users feel physically and mentally present within a virtual environment. These concepts are crucial for creating engaging and realistic VR experiences. Here's an explanation of presence and immersion in virtual environments:

1. Presence: Presence refers to the subjective feeling of "being there" in the virtual environment, as if the virtual world is a substitute for the physical world. It involves a sense of spatial presence, where users perceive themselves as existing within the virtual space. Presence can be influenced by factors such as realistic graphics, accurate spatial sound, and responsive interactions. When users experience a strong sense of presence, they tend to engage more deeply with the virtual environment and suspend their disbelief.

2. Immersion: Immersion is the degree to which users are engrossed and absorbed in the virtual environment. It encompasses both psychological immersion (mental engagement) and sensory immersion (perceptual stimuli). Psychological immersion relates to the level of mental involvement and attention given to the virtual experience. Sensory immersion involves the extent to which the user's senses are stimulated and aligned with the virtual world, including visual, auditory, and sometimes haptic (touch) feedback. Achieving a high level of immersion helps to create a compelling and realistic VR experience.

Presence and immersion are closely related and mutually reinforcing. When users feel a strong sense of presence, it enhances their feeling of immersion, and vice versa. Various technological factors contribute to creating a sense of presence and immersion, such as high-resolution displays, spatial audio, realistic physics simulations, and responsive tracking systems. Design elements such as interactive environments, compelling narratives, and engaging interactions also play a crucial role in promoting presence and immersion.

The goal of achieving presence and immersion in VR is to create a sense of believability and authenticity, allowing users to fully engage with the virtual world and have meaningful experiences. Presence and immersion are fundamental to the success of applications in gaming, training and simulations, virtual tourism, storytelling, and other fields where a deep level of user engagement is desired. Advances in technology and continued research in this area are driving the development of more immersive and compelling virtual experiences.

Ethical considerations and user well-being

Ethical considerations and user well-being are important aspects that need to be addressed in the development and implementation of virtual reality (VR) experiences. While VR has the potential to provide transformative and immersive experiences, it also raises certain ethical concerns that should be carefully considered. Here are some key ethical considerations in the context of VR:

1. Privacy and Data Protection: VR experiences often involve the collection and processing of personal data, such as biometric information and user behavior. It is essential to prioritize user privacy and implement robust data protection measures to ensure that users' personal information is securely stored and used only for intended purposes.

2. Informed Consent: Obtaining informed consent from users is crucial in VR experiences, particularly when sensitive data is being collected or when the experience involves potential risks. Users should be well-informed about the nature of the experience, any potential risks or side effects, and how their data will be used.

3. Physical and Psychological Safety: VR experiences have the potential to evoke strong emotional and physical responses. Developers should design experiences that prioritize user safety, taking into account factors such as motion sickness, eyestrain, and the potential for triggering anxiety or distressing reactions. Clear warnings and safety guidelines should be provided to users.

4. Accessibility and Inclusivity: Ensuring that VR experiences are accessible to a diverse range of users is essential. Developers should consider factors such as physical accessibility, support for different input devices, and accommodations for users with disabilities. Designing interfaces and interactions that are intuitive and inclusive can enhance the overall user experience.

5. Content and User Experience: VR content should adhere to ethical guidelines and avoid promoting harmful, discriminatory, or offensive content. Developers should consider the potential impact of the content on users' mental and emotional well-being, and strive to create experiences that are engaging, informative, and respectful of cultural sensitivities.

6. Addiction and Overuse: VR experiences can be highly immersive and engaging, which raises concerns about addiction and overuse. Developers should consider implementing mechanisms to encourage responsible use, such as providing usage statistics, incorporating breaks, and promoting a healthy balance between virtual and real-world experiences.

7. Ethical AI and Virtual Characters: If virtual characters or artificial intelligence (AI) are part of the VR experience, ethical considerations should be taken into account. This includes ensuring that virtual characters are designed and programmed to respect user boundaries, avoid promoting harmful behaviors, and uphold ethical standards.

By addressing these ethical considerations and prioritizing user well-being, developers can create VR experiences that are enjoyable, safe, inclusive, and respectful of users' rights and values. Collaboration between developers, researchers, policymakers, and user communities is essential in establishing ethical guidelines and standards for VR applications.

Addressing motion sickness and discomfort

Motion sickness and discomfort are common challenges associated with virtual reality (VR) experiences. These sensations occur when there is a disconnect between the visual cues provided by the VR headset and the user's physical movements or perceived lack of movement. Fortunately, there are strategies and techniques that can help address motion sickness and discomfort in VR:

1. Smooth Movement: Avoid rapid or jerky movements in VR experiences. Opt for smooth and gradual transitions when the user moves within the virtual environment. Sudden changes in perspective or acceleration can trigger motion sickness. Implementing techniques such as teleportation or using a virtual grid to guide movement can help reduce discomfort.

2. Field of View (FOV): Consider the user's field of view when designing VR experiences. A wide FOV can enhance immersion, but it can also increase the likelihood of motion sickness. Finding the right balance is crucial. Adjusting FOV settings based on the user's comfort level can help mitigate discomfort.

3. Reduce Latency: Minimize latency, which is the delay between a user's movement and the corresponding update in the VR display. High latency can contribute to motion sickness. Optimize the VR system's performance to ensure minimal delay between user actions and visual feedback.

4. Visual Cues and Anchors: Provide visual cues and reference points within the virtual environment to help

users maintain their sense of orientation and reduce disorientation. For example, including a fixed point of reference or using a cockpit-like interface can give users a stable frame of reference.

5. Gradual Exposure: If users are prone to motion sickness, consider gradually exposing them to more immersive VR experiences over time. Start with shorter sessions and gradually increase the duration as users build tolerance.

6. Comfortable Movement Options: Offer different movement options to cater to users with varying levels of sensitivity. For example, provide teleportation, smooth sliding, or joystick-based locomotion as alternatives, allowing users to choose the method that feels most comfortable to them.

7. Breaks and Rest Periods: Encourage users to take breaks during VR experiences, especially if they start feeling discomfort or motion sickness symptoms. Regular breaks can help prevent fatigue and reduce the likelihood of experiencing prolonged discomfort.

8. User Settings and Preferences: Allow users to customize certain settings, such as movement speed, comfort mode options, or vignettes that reduce peripheral vision during movement. Providing users with control over these settings allows them to adjust the VR experience according to their individual comfort levels.

It's important to note that individuals may have different sensitivities to motion sickness, so it's essential to offer flexibility and options within VR experiences to accommodate a broader range of users. Additionally, ongoing research and development in VR technology are continually improving motion tracking, display quality, and other factors that contribute to a more comfortable and immersive experience.

Virtual reality in the gaming industry

Virtual reality (VR) has revolutionized the gaming industry by providing immersive and interactive experiences that transport players into virtual worlds. Here are some key aspects of virtual reality in the gaming industry:

1. Immersive Gameplay: VR gaming offers a level of immersion that traditional gaming cannot replicate. Players can step into the shoes of their in-game characters and physically interact with the virtual environment. This heightened sense of presence enhances the overall gaming experience and creates a deeper connection between players and the virtual world.

2. Enhanced Interaction: With VR, players can use hand controllers, motion tracking devices, and haptic feedback systems to interact with the virtual environment and objects in a more intuitive and realistic manner. This allows for immersive gameplay mechanics, such as picking up and manipulating objects, throwing projectiles, or engaging in hand-to-hand combat.

3. Realistic Environments: VR technology enables the creation of highly realistic and visually stunning virtual environments. Players can explore fantastical worlds, historical settings, or futuristic landscapes with a sense of depth and scale that feels incredibly lifelike. This level of realism enhances the sense of wonder and adventure in gaming.

4. Multiplayer Experiences: VR gaming has also brought

about new possibilities for multiplayer experiences. Players can interact with other participants in the virtual world, engaging in cooperative or competitive gameplay. VR multiplayer games foster social connections and allow for shared experiences, whether it's teaming up to solve puzzles or engaging in intense virtual battles.

5. New Game Genres and Mechanics: VR has sparked the emergence of new game genres and mechanics that are tailor-made for immersive experiences. From puzzle-solving and exploration games to intense action and horror titles, VR offers unique gameplay mechanics that fully leverage the technology's capabilities. For example, players can physically duck behind cover, aim and shoot with precision, or navigate complex environments with natural movements.

6. Innovative Storytelling: Virtual reality has opened up new avenues for storytelling in gaming. Developers can create narratives that place players at the center of the action, allowing them to experience the story firsthand. The immersive nature of VR enhances emotional engagement and creates a more personal connection with the game's characters and narrative.

7. Accessible VR: Over time, VR technology has become more accessible to a wider audience. VR headsets have become more affordable, and there is a growing library of games and experiences available across different platforms. This accessibility has contributed to the broader adoption of VR in the gaming industry.

Virtual reality has revolutionized gaming by offering unprecedented levels of immersion, interaction, and realism. It continues to push the boundaries of what is possible in gaming, creating new and exciting experiences for players. As technology advances and VR adoption grows, we can expect even more innovative and compelling games to shape the future of the industry.

Virtual reality in healthcare and medicine

Virtual reality (VR) has made significant strides in the field of healthcare and medicine, transforming the way medical professionals deliver care and improving patient outcomes. Here are some key applications of virtual reality in healthcare:

1. Medical Training and Education: VR provides realistic simulations and training scenarios for medical students, residents, and practicing healthcare professionals. It allows them to practice procedures, surgical techniques, and emergency simulations in a safe and controlled virtual environment. VR training enhances skills development, improves clinical decision-making, and reduces the risk associated with real-life procedures.

2. Pain Management and Distraction: VR has proven to be an effective tool in managing pain and reducing anxiety during medical procedures. By immersing patients in virtual environments, it helps to distract them from the discomfort and pain associated with treatments, such as wound dressings, injections, or dental procedures. VR experiences can be tailored to each patient's preferences, providing calming and engaging content that promotes relaxation.

3. Rehabilitation and Physical Therapy: Virtual reality is used in rehabilitation and physical therapy to assist patients in regaining mobility, coordination, and motor skills. Through VR-based exercises and simulations, patients can perform interactive and engaging activities that promote movement and balance. Virtual reality

also allows therapists to track progress, customize treatment plans, and provide real-time feedback to patients.

4. Mental Health and Stress Management: VR is increasingly being utilized in mental health treatments, including anxiety disorders, phobias, post-traumatic stress disorder (PTSD), and other mental health conditions. Virtual environments provide controlled exposure therapy, allowing patients to face their fears in a safe and controlled manner. VR-based relaxation and mindfulness programs are also used to reduce stress, promote relaxation, and improve overall mental well-being.

5. Rehabilitation for Neurological Conditions: Virtual reality has shown promise in assisting patients with neurological conditions, such as stroke or traumatic brain injury, in their rehabilitation journey. VR-based exercises and simulations help improve motor skills, coordination, and cognitive function. It also provides a motivating and engaging environment for patients, enhancing their participation and adherence to rehabilitation programs.

6. Medical Visualization and Preoperative Planning: VR enables healthcare professionals to visualize complex medical data, such as medical imaging scans (MRI, CT), in three-dimensional virtual environments. This immersive visualization aids in preoperative planning, allowing surgeons to better understand patient anatomy and plan surgical procedures with increased precision. It can also be used for patient education, helping individuals better comprehend their condition and treatment options.

7. Telemedicine and Virtual Consultations: VR technology has the potential to enhance telemedicine experiences by providing a more immersive and interactive connection between healthcare providers and patients.

Virtual consultations and remote medical examinations can be conducted using VR, allowing healthcare professionals to remotely assess patients, provide guidance, and monitor progress.

Virtual reality has the potential to revolutionize healthcare by improving medical training, patient care, and therapeutic interventions. It offers immersive and personalized experiences that enhance engagement, reduce stress, and improve outcomes. As the technology continues to advance, we can expect to see further integration of virtual reality into various aspects of healthcare, ultimately leading to improved patient outcomes and enhanced medical practices.

Virtual reality in education and training

Virtual reality (VR) has emerged as a powerful tool in the field of education and training, revolutionizing the way we learn and acquire new skills. Here are some key applications of virtual reality in education and training:

1. Immersive Learning Environments: VR creates realistic and immersive environments that enhance the learning experience. Students can explore historical sites, dive into scientific simulations, or travel to distant locations, all from the comfort of their classrooms. This immersive learning fosters engagement, curiosity, and a deeper understanding of the subject matter.

2. Virtual Field Trips: VR allows students to go on virtual field trips to places that might be otherwise inaccessible. They can visit famous landmarks, explore ecosystems, or even embark on virtual space expeditions. Virtual field trips provide a rich and interactive learning experience, expanding students' horizons and broadening their perspectives.

3. Practical Skills Training: VR enables hands-on training in various fields, such as medicine, engineering, and vocational trades. Students can practice surgical procedures, assemble machinery, or simulate real-life scenarios in a safe and controlled environment. This practical training enhances skills development, promotes critical thinking, and improves muscle memory.

4. Simulation-based Learning: VR simulations provide opportunities for students to apply their knowledge

in realistic scenarios. They can practice problem-solving, decision-making, and teamwork in virtual environments that closely mimic real-world situations. This experiential learning approach enhances skills transfer and prepares students for real-life challenges.

5. Language Learning and Cultural Immersion: VR facilitates language learning by immersing students in virtual environments where they can practice conversational skills, engage in language activities, and interact with virtual native speakers. It also enables cultural immersion, allowing students to experience different cultures, customs, and traditions firsthand.

6. Special Education and Inclusion: VR has proven to be beneficial for students with special needs by providing customized and inclusive learning experiences. It can create sensory-rich environments, cater to individual learning styles, and offer interactive simulations that accommodate different abilities and preferences. VR promotes inclusivity and equal access to education for all students.

7. Teacher Training and Professional Development: VR offers opportunities for teacher training and professional development. Educators can participate in virtual workshops, observe exemplary teaching practices, and collaborate with colleagues from around the world. VR-based training enhances teaching methodologies, encourages innovation, and supports continuous professional growth.

Virtual reality has the potential to transform education and training by providing immersive, interactive, and personalized learning experiences. It engages students, enhances retention, and promotes active participation. As the technology continues to advance, we can expect to see broader integration of virtual reality into educational institutions, training programs, and lifelong learning initiatives, ultimately revolutionizing the way we acquire knowledge and skills.

Virtual reality in architecture and design

Virtual reality (VR) has significantly impacted the field of architecture and design, revolutionizing the way professionals conceptualize, visualize, and communicate their ideas. Here are some key applications of virtual reality in architecture and design:

1. Design Visualization: VR allows architects and designers to create immersive virtual environments that bring their designs to life. By putting on a VR headset, clients and stakeholders can experience a virtual walkthrough of a building or space before it is constructed. This enhances the understanding of the design, helps identify potential issues, and enables stakeholders to provide valuable feedback at an early stage.

2. Spatial Planning and Layout: VR enables architects and designers to experiment with different spatial configurations and layouts. They can create virtual 3D models of buildings or spaces, arrange furniture, test lighting scenarios, and assess the overall aesthetics and functionality. This iterative design process helps optimize the use of space and facilitates informed decision-making.

3. Material and Finish Selection: VR allows architects and designers to visualize different materials, textures, and finishes in a virtual environment. They can simulate how different materials look and feel, explore various color schemes, and evaluate the visual impact of different design choices. This virtual material selection process saves time, reduces costs, and enables better-informed decisions.

4. Client Presentations and Communication: VR enhances the communication between architects, designers, and clients. Instead of relying on traditional 2D drawings or renderings, VR provides an immersive platform for clients to experience and understand the proposed designs. They can navigate through virtual spaces, interact with objects, and gain a realistic sense of scale and proportion. This immersive experience fosters clearer communication and aligns client expectations with the final design.

5. Collaborative Design Reviews: VR facilitates collaborative design reviews among architects, designers, engineers, and other stakeholders. Multiple participants can join a shared virtual environment, explore the design together, and provide real-time feedback. This collaborative design process streamlines decision-making, improves coordination, and enhances the overall quality of the design.

6. Sustainable Design and Analysis: VR can be utilized to analyze and optimize sustainable design strategies. Architects can simulate daylighting conditions, assess energy efficiency, and analyze the environmental impact of design choices. VR-based simulations enable architects to make data-driven decisions that contribute to sustainable and environmentally friendly design practices.

7. Architectural Education and Training: VR is increasingly used in architectural education to enhance learning experiences. Students can explore architectural masterpieces, study historical buildings, and engage in design studios within virtual environments. VR-based education provides a hands-on, immersive approach that fosters creativity, critical thinking, and spatial understanding.

Virtual reality has transformed the architectural and design industries by providing immersive and interactive tools for design visualization, client communication, collaboration, and sustainable design analysis. As the technology continues to advance, we can expect further integration of VR into design workflows, enabling architects and designers to push the boundaries of creativity, improve design outcomes, and create more engaging and sustainable built environments.

Virtual reality in the entertainment industry

Virtual reality (VR) has had a significant impact on the entertainment industry, revolutionizing the way we consume and experience media. Here are some key applications of virtual reality in the entertainment industry:

1. Immersive Gaming: Virtual reality gaming provides players with a truly immersive and interactive experience. With VR headsets and motion controllers, gamers can step into virtual worlds, physically move around, and interact with objects and characters in a more realistic way. VR gaming offers a heightened sense of presence and engagement, creating experiences that are highly immersive and memorable.

2. Cinematic VR Experiences: Virtual reality has opened up new possibilities for storytelling in the realm of film and video. VR cinematic experiences allow viewers to be fully immersed in a narrative, feeling like they are present within the story. Filmmakers and content creators can utilize VR to transport audiences to new environments, provide unique perspectives, and create emotionally impactful experiences.

3. Live Events and Concerts: Virtual reality enables remote attendance of live events and concerts, breaking the barriers of physical distance. With VR, users can watch live performances, sports events, and other entertainment experiences from the comfort of their homes, feeling as if they are actually present at the venue. This opens up opportunities for wider audience reach and new revenue streams for event organizers.

4. Virtual Theme Parks and Attractions: VR has enhanced the theme park experience by offering immersive rides and attractions. Virtual reality can transport visitors to fantasy worlds, simulate thrilling adventures, and provide interactive and dynamic experiences. Theme parks and entertainment venues are incorporating VR technology to create innovative and memorable experiences that blend physical and virtual elements.

5. Virtual Reality Arcades: Dedicated VR arcades and gaming centers have emerged, offering a social and shared VR experience. These spaces provide access to high-end VR equipment and a variety of games and experiences that may not be easily accessible at home. VR arcades offer a social environment for friends and families to come together and enjoy immersive gaming and entertainment.

6. Virtual Reality Filmmaking and Production: VR technology is being utilized in the production and creation of immersive content. Filmmakers and content creators are experimenting with VR cameras and techniques to capture 360-degree videos and experiences. This opens up new avenues for creative expression and storytelling, pushing the boundaries of traditional filmmaking.

7. Virtual Reality Experiences in Museums and Exhibitions: Museums and cultural institutions are incorporating VR to enhance visitors' experiences. VR allows users to explore historical sites, visit museums remotely, and interact with virtual artifacts and exhibitions. This expands access to cultural heritage and provides interactive and educational experiences that go beyond traditional exhibits.

Virtual reality has transformed the entertainment industry by providing immersive and interactive experiences that transport users to new worlds and engage their senses. As the technology continues to advance, we can expect more innovative and compelling applications of virtual reality in gaming, film, live events, theme parks, and other entertainment mediums, shaping the future of entertainment and storytelling.

Virtual reality in marketing and advertising

Virtual reality (VR) has opened up exciting possibilities for marketing and advertising, allowing brands to create immersive and engaging experiences for their target audience. Here are some key ways virtual reality is being used in the marketing and advertising industry:

1. Product Demonstrations and Experiences: VR enables brands to showcase their products or services in a virtual environment, providing customers with interactive and realistic experiences. Whether it's test-driving a car, trying on virtual fashion items, or exploring a virtual property, VR allows potential customers to fully engage with products before making a purchase decision.

2. Virtual Showrooms and Retail Spaces: Virtual reality can recreate physical retail environments in the virtual realm, providing customers with a virtual showroom experience. Brands can create immersive virtual stores where customers can browse products, interact with virtual sales representatives, and make purchases. This allows brands to reach a wider audience and create unique shopping experiences.

3. Brand Storytelling and Immersive Campaigns: VR enables brands to tell their stories in a more immersive and memorable way. Brands can create virtual experiences that transport customers to different worlds, engage them emotionally, and leave a lasting impression. Whether it's taking customers on a virtual tour of their brand's history or creating a branded VR

game, virtual reality allows for creative and impactful storytelling.

4. Virtual Events and Sponsorships: Virtual reality offers opportunities for brands to sponsor or host virtual events, such as conferences, trade shows, or concerts. Brands can create virtual environments where participants can network, attend sessions, and engage with branded content. Virtual sponsorships allow for increased brand visibility and interaction with a global audience.

5. Data Collection and Customer Insights: Virtual reality experiences can provide valuable data and insights for marketers. By tracking user interactions within the virtual environment, brands can gather data on customer preferences, behavior, and engagement. This data can be used to refine marketing strategies, personalize offerings, and improve the overall customer experience.

6. Brand Activation and Experiential Marketing: VR can be utilized for brand activations and experiential marketing campaigns. Brands can create immersive experiences at events, trade shows, or pop-up stores, attracting and engaging audiences in unique ways. VR activations can generate buzz, increase brand awareness, and create shareable content that extends the reach of the campaign.

7. Virtual Reality Advertising: Brands can develop virtual reality ad campaigns that appear within VR experiences or VR content platforms. These ads can be interactive and engaging, allowing users to explore branded content and products within the virtual environment. Virtual reality ads provide an innovative way for brands to capture the attention of consumers and deliver impactful messages.

Virtual reality has transformed the marketing and advertising landscape by providing brands with new avenues to engage and connect with their target audience. By leveraging the immersive and interactive nature of VR, marketers can create memorable experiences, tell compelling brand stories, and drive customer engagement. As virtual reality technology continues to advance, we can expect even more innovative and immersive marketing experiences that blur the line between the physical and digital realms.

3D modeling and animation for virtual environments

3D modeling and animation play a crucial role in creating immersive virtual environments in virtual reality (VR). Here's an overview of how 3D modeling and animation contribute to the development of virtual environments:

1. Virtual Environment Creation: 3D modeling is used to create the virtual objects, structures, and landscapes that make up the virtual environment. Artists and designers use specialized software to create detailed 3D models of buildings, landscapes, furniture, props, and other elements that populate the virtual world. These 3D models are then textured, lit, and arranged within the virtual space to create a realistic and visually appealing environment.

2. Object Interactions and Physics Simulation: In virtual environments, objects need to interact with each other and respond to user input. 3D modeling and animation techniques are used to define the physics properties of objects, such as weight, collision detection, and motion. Through physics simulation, objects can realistically collide, bounce, and move within the virtual environment, providing a sense of realism and immersion for users.

3. Character Creation and Animation: Virtual environments often include virtual characters or avatars that users can interact with. 3D modeling is used to create detailed character models, including

their appearance, clothing, and accessories. Animation techniques are then applied to bring these characters to life. Animators create skeletal structures for the characters and define their movements, expressions, and gestures. This allows users to interact with lifelike and expressive virtual characters within the virtual environment.

4. Environmental Effects and Atmosphere: 3D modeling and animation also contribute to creating realistic environmental effects and atmosphere in virtual environments. This includes modeling and animating weather conditions like rain, snow, or fog, as well as lighting effects such as dynamic shadows, reflections, and particle systems. These elements enhance the overall visual quality and immersion of the virtual environment, making it more engaging for users.

5. User Interface and Interaction Design: 3D modeling and animation are used to design and create user interfaces (UI) within the virtual environment. This includes creating 3D buttons, menus, and interactive elements that users can interact with using VR controllers or gestures. Animations are employed to provide feedback and visual cues to guide users through the virtual environment and enhance the overall user experience.

6. Cinematic and Narrative Experiences: 3D modeling and animation techniques are used to create cinematic and narrative experiences within virtual environments. This involves creating scripted sequences, cutscenes, and storytelling elements that unfold as users navigate through the virtual space. By employing cinematic techniques such as camera movements, lighting, and visual effects, developers can create compelling and immersive narratives that enhance the user's sense of immersion and engagement.

In summary, 3D modeling and animation are essential

components of virtual reality development, enabling the creation of detailed virtual objects, realistic environments, interactive characters, and immersive experiences. These techniques bring virtual environments to life, providing users with engaging and interactive virtual experiences that bridge the gap between the digital and physical worlds.

Interactive storytelling in virtual reality

Interactive storytelling in virtual reality (VR) combines the power of narrative with the immersive nature of VR technology, allowing users to become active participants in the storytelling experience. It offers a unique and compelling way to engage audiences, providing them with agency and the ability to shape the narrative through their actions and choices. Here are some key aspects of interactive storytelling in VR:

1. Immersive Narrative Experiences: VR allows users to step into the story and become part of the virtual world. They can explore the environment, interact with objects and characters, and make choices that influence the story's progression. This level of immersion enhances the emotional impact of the narrative and creates a stronger connection between the user and the story.

2. Non-Linear Storytelling: In VR, traditional linear narratives can be expanded to include non-linear storytelling elements. Users can navigate through different story paths, uncover hidden narratives, and make choices that lead to different outcomes. This interactive aspect gives users a sense of agency and personalization, making the story feel more dynamic and engaging.

3. Branching Narratives: Interactive storytelling in VR often incorporates branching narratives, where the story diverges based on the user's choices and actions. These branches can lead to different story arcs, character interactions, and outcomes. Users may experience multiple endings or variations of the story,

adding to the replay value and creating a sense of discovery.

4. Environmental Storytelling: VR provides an opportunity to tell stories through the environment itself. Details, objects, and visual cues within the virtual space can convey narrative elements, backstory, and world-building. Users can actively explore and uncover these elements, deepening their understanding of the narrative world.

5. Spatial Audio and Sound Design: Sound plays a crucial role in immersive storytelling in VR. Spatial audio techniques enhance the sense of presence and realism, allowing users to locate sounds in 3D space. This helps in guiding attention, creating atmosphere, and providing auditory cues for narrative progression.

6. Character Interaction and Engagement: In VR, users can directly interact with virtual characters, engage in conversations, and affect the story through their interactions. This creates opportunities for emotional connections with the characters and a deeper sense of immersion in the narrative.

7. Time and Scale Manipulation: VR technology enables unique storytelling techniques such as time manipulation and scale changes. Users can witness events from different perspectives, travel through time, or experience the narrative on a grand or intimate scale. These techniques add layers of complexity and intrigue to the storytelling experience.

8. Multiplayer and Social Experiences: VR allows for multiplayer and social interactions within the virtual environment. Users can collaborate, compete, or engage with other participants, creating shared narrative experiences. This opens up possibilities for collaborative storytelling, social exploration, and collective decision-making.

Interactive storytelling in VR pushes the boundaries of traditional storytelling by immersing users in rich and dynamic narrative experiences. It empowers users to actively engage with the story, influencing its direction and outcomes. With its unique capabilities, VR provides an exciting platform for innovative and immersive storytelling that captivates audiences in entirely new ways.

User interface and user experience design in virtual reality

User interface (UI) and user experience (UX) design in virtual reality (VR) play a crucial role in creating immersive and intuitive experiences for users. In VR, the design of UI and UX needs to consider the unique challenges and opportunities presented by the virtual environment. Here are some key considerations for UI and UX design in VR:

1. Spatial Design: VR environments have three-dimensional space, and UI elements need to be placed and designed accordingly. Spatial design involves placing UI elements in the virtual space to ensure visibility, accessibility, and usability. Careful consideration should be given to the size, position, and orientation of UI elements to avoid obstructing the user's view or causing discomfort.

2. Immersive Interactions: VR provides the opportunity for natural and immersive interactions. UI elements should be designed to leverage the capabilities of VR controllers or hand tracking, allowing users to interact with objects and menus in a seamless and intuitive manner. Gestural interactions, such as grabbing and manipulating objects, enhance the sense of presence and immersion.

3. Visual Hierarchy and Clarity: In VR, it's important to guide the user's attention effectively. Clear visual hierarchy ensures that important UI elements are easily noticeable and distinguishable. Color, contrast, size, and

animation can be used to draw attention and provide visual cues for navigation and interaction.

4. Minimalism and Simplicity: Due to limited screen space in VR, UI design should aim for simplicity and minimalism. Avoid cluttering the user's view with excessive information or complex UI elements. Strive for a clean and unobtrusive design that prioritizes essential information and functionality.

5. Feedback and Responsiveness: Providing immediate and responsive feedback is crucial in VR. Users should receive visual, auditory, and haptic feedback when interacting with UI elements, confirming their actions and ensuring a sense of control and engagement. Feedback can include animations, sound effects, and haptic vibrations to enhance the overall experience.

6. Comfort and Ergonomics: VR experiences should prioritize user comfort and minimize any potential discomfort or motion sickness. UI design should consider factors such as text legibility, font size, and user interface placement to minimize eye strain and fatigue. Smooth transitions, comfortable movement, and well-designed locomotion mechanisms contribute to a comfortable user experience.

7. User Testing and Iteration: Iterative user testing is essential in VR UI/UX design. Collecting feedback from users and incorporating their insights helps identify usability issues, improve interaction flows, and optimize the overall user experience. Regular testing and iteration ensure that the UI/UX design aligns with user expectations and preferences.

8. Contextual Guidance and Onboarding: As VR experiences can be novel for many users, providing contextual guidance and intuitive onboarding is essential. Clear instructions, tooltips, or interactive tutorials can help users understand the UI and interaction mechanics, ensuring a smooth and engaging

experience from the start.

Effective UI and UX design in VR should aim to create intuitive, immersive, and user-friendly experiences. By considering spatial design, immersive interactions, visual hierarchy, responsiveness, comfort, and user testing, designers can create compelling and enjoyable VR experiences that captivate and engage users.

Sound design and spatial audio in virtual reality

Sound design and spatial audio play a crucial role in enhancing the immersive experience of virtual reality (VR). In VR, audio adds depth, realism, and a sense of presence to the virtual environment. Here are some key considerations for sound design and spatial audio in VR:

1. Spatial Audio: Spatial audio refers to the ability to reproduce sound in a three-dimensional space, providing users with a sense of direction, distance, and location of sound sources within the VR environment. By using head-related transfer functions (HRTFs) and binaural rendering techniques, audio can be rendered to simulate the way sound behaves in the real world, creating a realistic and immersive auditory experience.

2. Object-based Audio: Object-based audio allows individual audio sources to be treated as separate objects in the virtual space. Each sound object can have its own position, movement, and characteristics, enabling dynamic and interactive audio experiences. Object-based audio enhances realism and enables realistic sound propagation and occlusion, where sounds are affected by virtual objects and their positions.

3. Ambisonics: Ambisonics is a spatial audio format that captures sound from all directions using a spherical microphone array. Ambisonics recordings can be used to create an immersive sound field within the VR environment. By decoding Ambisonics recordings and

rendering them in real-time, users can experience a rich and detailed soundscape that enhances their sense of presence and immersion.

4. Environmental Audio: VR environments often have dynamic and interactive elements, such as moving objects, weather effects, or spatial triggers. Environmental audio design involves creating audio cues and responses that correspond to these environmental changes. For example, as the user moves through the virtual space, the audio should adapt and respond to their location, providing a seamless and cohesive audio experience.

5. Sound Effects and Foley: Sound effects and foley play an important role in creating a realistic and immersive VR experience. Every interaction, object movement, or environmental element should have corresponding audio effects to enhance the sense of presence and realism. Attention to detail in sound design can greatly contribute to the overall immersion and user engagement in the virtual environment.

6. User Interface (UI) Audio: UI audio refers to the sounds associated with user interactions, such as button clicks, menu navigation, or feedback for actions. Thoughtful and well-designed UI audio can provide important auditory feedback to users, helping them understand their interactions and providing a more engaging and responsive user experience.

7. Emotional and Narrative Impact: Sound has the ability to evoke emotions and enhance storytelling. In VR experiences, audio cues, music, and voice-over narration can significantly impact the user's emotional engagement and narrative immersion. By carefully crafting audio elements to align with the desired emotional tone and narrative arc, creators can evoke specific feelings and enhance the overall impact of the VR experience.

8. Audio Optimization: VR experiences are often delivered on various platforms with different hardware capabilities. Optimizing audio assets and implementation is crucial to ensure optimal performance and audio quality across different devices and platforms. Compression techniques, audio streaming, and adaptive audio solutions can be employed to provide the best possible audio experience while maintaining performance efficiency.

Sound design and spatial audio are integral components of the immersive VR experience. By leveraging techniques such as spatial audio rendering, object-based audio, environmental audio design, and careful attention to detail, creators can enhance the sense of presence, realism, and emotional impact in the virtual environment, resulting in a more immersive and engaging VR experience for users.

Hardware limitations and affordability

Hardware limitations and affordability have been significant factors influencing the widespread adoption of virtual reality (VR). While VR technology has made significant advancements in recent years, there are still considerations related to hardware requirements and cost that impact its accessibility to a broader audience. Here are some key points regarding hardware limitations and affordability in VR:

1. High-performance Requirements: VR experiences typically demand powerful hardware to deliver a smooth and immersive experience. This includes a high-resolution display, fast refresh rates, and accurate motion tracking. These requirements can limit the accessibility of VR to users who may not have access to or cannot afford the necessary hardware.

2. PC and Console Requirements: Many VR systems, such as the Oculus Rift or HTC Vive, require a compatible gaming PC or gaming console to run the VR applications. These systems can be costly, and not everyone may already have the necessary hardware specifications to support VR experiences. This adds an additional financial barrier to entry for potential VR users.

3. Standalone VR Headsets: In recent years, standalone VR headsets, such as the Oculus Quest, have emerged as more accessible options. These headsets do not require a separate gaming PC or console and are generally more affordable. However, they may have limitations in terms of processing power, graphics quality, and overall performance compared to PC-based VR systems.

4. Mobile VR: Mobile VR offers a more affordable entry point into VR experiences as it utilizes smartphones and compatible VR headsets, such as Google Cardboard or Samsung Gear VR. While mobile VR provides a cost-effective option, it may have limitations in terms of graphical fidelity and processing power, resulting in a less immersive experience compared to PC-based or standalone VR.

5. Price Reductions and Market Competition: As VR technology advances and competition increases, there is a trend of price reductions for VR hardware. Companies are working towards offering more affordable options to make VR accessible to a wider audience. This includes both standalone headsets and PC-based systems, with the aim of reducing the overall cost and hardware requirements.

6. Second-hand Market: Another consideration for affordability is the availability of second-hand VR equipment. As early adopters upgrade their hardware, older models may become available at lower prices on the second-hand market, making VR more accessible to budget-conscious users.

7. Innovation and Technological Advancements: Continued innovation in VR technology is likely to lead to advancements that address hardware limitations and cost. This includes improvements in display technology, processing power, and overall efficiency, making VR more accessible and affordable over time.

While hardware limitations and affordability remain challenges, the VR industry is actively working towards addressing these issues to make VR more accessible to a wider range of users. As technology progresses, we can expect to see improvements in affordability, performance, and accessibility, ultimately driving the broader adoption of VR experiences across various industries and user demographics.

User comfort and health considerations

User comfort and health considerations are crucial aspects of virtual reality (VR) experiences. While VR offers immersive and engaging experiences, it is important to prioritize the well-being and comfort of users. Here are some key considerations:

1. Motion Sickness: Motion sickness can occur when there is a disconnect between what users see in the VR environment and the movement or lack of movement they feel in the physical world. This can lead to symptoms such as nausea, dizziness, and discomfort. Developers and designers must implement techniques to minimize motion sickness, such as smooth locomotion, reducing latency, and providing comfort settings that allow users to adjust their experience based on their tolerance levels.

2. Eye Strain and Fatigue: Extended periods of VR use can lead to eye strain and fatigue due to the close proximity of the display to the eyes and the constant focus adjustment required. To mitigate these issues, VR systems should have high-quality displays with appropriate resolution, refresh rates, and optics. It is also important to encourage users to take breaks and limit the duration of VR sessions.

3. Physical Comfort: VR headsets can vary in terms of weight, fit, and adjustability. Ensuring a comfortable and secure fit is essential to prevent discomfort or pain during prolonged use. Adjustable straps, cushioning, and ergonomic designs can contribute to a better user experience. Additionally, considering the weight

distribution of the headset and minimizing pressure on the face and head can improve comfort.

4. Hygiene and Sanitization: Shared VR headsets or controllers in public settings raise concerns about hygiene. Regular cleaning and sanitization protocols should be established to maintain cleanliness and reduce the spread of germs. This can include using disposable face covers or providing easy-to-clean materials for headsets and controllers.

5. Physical Safety: Creating a safe environment for VR experiences is crucial. Users should have enough space to move around without obstacles or hazards that could lead to accidents. Providing clear instructions and guidelines on how to use the VR equipment safely can help prevent injuries.

6. Accessibility: Considerations for accessibility are essential to ensure that VR experiences are inclusive and can be enjoyed by users with varying abilities. This includes providing options for adjustable font sizes, closed captioning, color contrast settings, and accommodating different mobility needs.

7. User Education: Educating users about best practices for VR usage, including taking breaks, setting up a comfortable play area, and adjusting settings to their comfort level, can help promote a positive and safe experience.

As the VR industry continues to evolve, developers, designers, and manufacturers should prioritize user comfort and health. By addressing these considerations, VR experiences can be more enjoyable, inclusive, and accessible to a wider range of users, ultimately driving the widespread adoption of VR technology.

Content accessibility and inclusivity

Content accessibility and inclusivity are crucial aspects of virtual reality (VR) experiences. By ensuring that VR content is accessible to a wide range of users, we can create more inclusive and engaging virtual environments. Here are some key considerations for content accessibility and inclusivity in VR:

1. Visual Accessibility: Provide options for adjustable font sizes, color contrast settings, and customizable visual settings to accommodate users with visual impairments or color vision deficiencies. This can enhance readability and ensure that important information is accessible to all users.

2. Auditory Accessibility: Incorporate closed captioning or subtitles for audio elements in VR experiences to assist users with hearing impairments. Spatial audio techniques can be used to provide directional audio cues, allowing users to perceive sound and navigate the virtual environment effectively.

3. Motor Accessibility: Design interactions and controls in VR experiences to be adaptable and customizable. Provide options for different input methods, such as hand gestures, voice commands, or game controllers, to accommodate users with varying motor abilities. Consider implementing assistive technologies, such as head-tracking or eye-tracking, to enable users with limited mobility to interact with the VR environment.

4. Cognitive Accessibility: Create clear and intuitive user interfaces with consistent design patterns and minimal cognitive load. Avoid overwhelming users with

excessive visual or auditory stimuli and provide clear instructions or prompts within the VR experience. Consider providing additional support or guidance for users who may require it.

5. Language and Localization: Support multiple languages and localization options to make VR content accessible to users worldwide. This can involve providing language selection menus, multilingual interfaces, and localized content, such as text translations or voiceovers.

6. User Testing and Feedback: Conduct user testing with a diverse group of individuals, including those with disabilities or specific accessibility needs. Incorporate their feedback to improve the accessibility and inclusivity of VR content. Encourage users to provide feedback on their experience to help identify and address any accessibility barriers.

7. Awareness and Education: Raise awareness about the importance of accessibility and inclusivity in VR experiences among developers, designers, and content creators. Promote best practices and guidelines for creating accessible VR content, and provide resources and training to support the implementation of accessibility features.

By considering these aspects of content accessibility and inclusivity, we can ensure that VR experiences are accessible to a broader range of users, including those with disabilities or specific accessibility needs. This promotes equal participation and engagement in the virtual world, fostering a more inclusive and immersive VR ecosystem.

Ethical and privacy concerns

Ethical and privacy concerns are important considerations in the development and use of virtual reality (VR) technologies. As VR continues to evolve and become more integrated into our lives, it is crucial to address these concerns to ensure the responsible and ethical use of the technology. Here are some key ethical and privacy considerations in the context of VR:

1. Data Privacy: VR systems often collect and store user data, including personal information and behavioral data. It is important to have clear and transparent data privacy policies in place to protect user privacy. This includes informing users about what data is being collected, how it will be used, and providing options for users to control their data.

2. Informed Consent: Obtaining informed consent from users is essential in VR experiences, especially when sensitive data or personal information is involved. Users should be fully aware of the data collection practices, potential risks, and how their data will be used before engaging in VR experiences.

3. User Safety: VR experiences can create intense and immersive environments that may impact users emotionally and physically. Developers and content creators should prioritize user safety by providing clear warnings and guidelines for safe use, minimizing potential risks, and considering the physical and emotional well-being of users.

4. Accessibility and Inclusivity: Ensuring that VR experiences are accessible and inclusive to all

individuals, including those with disabilities or special needs, is an ethical responsibility. Designers and developers should consider the diverse range of users and create experiences that can be enjoyed by everyone, providing necessary accommodations and accessibility features.

5. Content and Ethical Representation: VR content should be created with ethical considerations in mind, avoiding content that promotes harm, discrimination, or unethical behavior. It is important to foster positive and inclusive experiences that respect cultural sensitivities and promote ethical values.

6. Virtual Harassment and Bullying: VR environments can create opportunities for virtual harassment and bullying. Developers and platform providers should implement measures to prevent and address instances of harassment, such as reporting mechanisms and moderation tools.

7. Consent and User Agency: Users should have control over their VR experiences and be able to provide explicit consent for actions or interactions. Designers and developers should prioritize user agency and avoid manipulative or coercive techniques.

8. Ethical AI and Virtual Characters: VR experiences may involve virtual characters or artificial intelligence systems. It is important to consider the ethical implications of these systems, including issues of consent, privacy, and the potential for bias or discrimination in AI algorithms.

9. Research and Ethical Guidelines: Researchers conducting studies in VR should follow ethical guidelines, ensuring participant safety, informed consent, and data protection. Ethical considerations should be integrated into the research process to prevent harm and respect the rights of participants.

By addressing these ethical and privacy concerns, we can foster a responsible and trustworthy VR ecosystem that respects user privacy, promotes inclusivity, and prioritizes ethical considerations in content creation and user experiences. It is important for stakeholders in the VR industry, including developers, researchers, policymakers, and users, to collaborate and establish standards and best practices that uphold ethical values and protect user rights.

Legal and regulatory challenges

Legal and regulatory challenges are significant considerations in the development and adoption of virtual reality (VR) technologies. As VR becomes more prevalent in various industries and everyday life, it is essential to navigate the legal landscape to ensure compliance, protect user rights, and address potential risks. Here are some key legal and regulatory challenges associated with VR:

1. Intellectual Property: VR content, including virtual environments, characters, and interactive experiences, may raise intellectual property concerns. This includes issues such as copyright, trademark, and patent infringement. Developers and content creators should understand and respect intellectual property rights, obtaining necessary permissions or licenses for the use of copyrighted material and avoiding infringement.

2. Privacy and Data Protection: VR systems often collect and process user data, including personal information and behavioral data. Compliance with privacy and data protection laws, such as the General Data Protection Regulation (GDPR) in the European Union, is crucial to safeguard user privacy. VR companies should implement robust data protection measures, including clear data privacy policies, consent mechanisms, and data security practices.

3. Consumer Protection: As VR technology becomes more accessible to consumers, it is important to protect users from fraudulent practices, misleading claims, and inadequate product safety. Consumer protection laws

and regulations need to be considered to ensure fair and transparent practices in marketing, sales, and product safety standards.

4. Content Regulation: VR content may raise concerns related to violence, explicit or inappropriate material, hate speech, or other potentially harmful content. Jurisdictions have different regulations and standards for content classification, labeling, and age restrictions. VR platforms and content creators should comply with applicable regulations and implement content moderation mechanisms to ensure responsible and appropriate experiences.

5. Health and Safety Regulations: VR experiences can have physical and psychological effects on users. It is important to consider health and safety regulations to ensure that VR systems and experiences adhere to industry standards and guidelines. This includes considerations for ergonomic design, risk assessment, and warnings about potential risks associated with VR use.

6. Employment and Labor Laws: The use of VR in workplaces, such as for training or remote collaboration, may have implications for employment and labor laws. Employers should ensure compliance with applicable laws, including those related to employee health and safety, data privacy, and the protection of workers' rights.

7. Liability and Insurance: As VR experiences involve user interaction and immersion, there may be potential risks and liability concerns. Developers, manufacturers, and platform providers should assess and mitigate risks, and consider appropriate liability and insurance coverage to protect against potential claims arising from VR-related incidents.

8. International Regulations: VR technologies are not confined by geographic boundaries, making

international regulations and compliance complex. Companies operating in multiple jurisdictions should be aware of regional regulations, cross-border data transfer restrictions, and compliance requirements to ensure global compliance.

9. Standardization and Industry Guidelines: As the VR industry evolves, establishing standards and industry guidelines can promote best practices and ensure consistent quality and safety standards. Collaboration among industry stakeholders, including VR companies, researchers, policymakers, and standardization organizations, is important for establishing guidelines and addressing emerging legal and regulatory challenges.

It is essential for VR stakeholders to stay informed about the legal and regulatory landscape, engage in responsible practices, and work towards establishing industry standards that prioritize user safety, privacy, and compliance. Close collaboration between industry players and regulatory bodies is necessary to navigate these challenges effectively and create an environment that fosters innovation while safeguarding user rights.

Emerging trends and technologies in virtual reality

Virtual reality (VR) continues to evolve at a rapid pace, driven by advancements in technology and the exploration of new possibilities. Several emerging trends and technologies are shaping the future of VR. Here are some notable ones:

1. Wireless and Standalone VR: Wireless and standalone VR systems are gaining popularity, eliminating the need for cumbersome cables and external hardware. These systems offer freedom of movement, ease of setup, and accessibility, making VR experiences more convenient and user-friendly.

2. Inside-Out Tracking: Inside-out tracking technologies enable VR headsets to track the user's movement and position without the need for external sensors. This technology enhances mobility and allows for more flexibility in setting up VR experiences, as users are not constrained by the placement of sensors.

3. Eye-Tracking and Foveated Rendering: Eye-tracking technology allows VR systems to monitor and track the user's eye movements. This enables more realistic and immersive experiences by dynamically rendering the highest level of detail in the user's line of sight, known as foveated rendering. Eye-tracking also opens up possibilities for interactive gaze-based interactions within VR environments.

4. Haptic Feedback and Sensory Integration: Advancements in haptic feedback systems are enabling

more realistic touch and tactile sensations in VR experiences. Haptic gloves, vests, and controllers provide users with a sense of touch and feedback, enhancing immersion and interaction within virtual environments. Integration of other sensory modalities, such as smell and temperature, is also being explored to create more multisensory VR experiences.

5. Social VR and Shared Experiences: Social VR platforms and applications are emerging, allowing users to connect and interact with others in virtual spaces. These platforms enable shared experiences, collaborative activities, and social interactions, making VR more engaging and sociable. From virtual meetings and events to multiplayer gaming, social VR is transforming how people connect and communicate.

6. Augmented Reality (AR) and Mixed Reality (MR) Integration: The convergence of VR with augmented reality (AR) and mixed reality (MR) technologies is blurring the lines between the physical and virtual worlds. Combining real-world elements with virtual objects and environments opens up new possibilities for interactive and immersive experiences that blend the best of both worlds.

7. AI and Machine Learning: AI and machine learning are being leveraged to enhance VR experiences. AI algorithms can be used for various purposes, such as improving natural language processing and speech recognition in VR applications, creating more realistic virtual characters and behaviors, and generating dynamic and adaptive content based on user interactions and preferences.

8. Cloud-Based VR: Cloud computing is playing a significant role in expanding the capabilities of VR. Cloud-based VR solutions offload the processing power and storage requirements to remote servers, allowing for more complex and resource-intensive

VR experiences without the need for high-end local hardware. This enables VR accessibility on lower-end devices and promotes broader adoption.

9. Virtual Reality for Training and Simulation: VR is increasingly being adopted for training and simulation purposes across industries such as healthcare, aviation, manufacturing, and defense. Immersive VR environments provide a safe and controlled space for trainees to practice and refine their skills, reducing costs and risks associated with real-world training scenarios.

10. Content Creation Tools and User-generated Content: The democratization of VR content creation is empowering users to create and share their virtual experiences. User-friendly content creation tools and platforms are emerging, allowing individuals with minimal technical expertise to design and publish VR content. User-generated content fosters creativity, diversity, and a vibrant VR community.

These emerging trends and technologies demonstrate the ongoing innovation and potential of virtual reality. As the technology continues to advance, it is expected to impact various industries, transform entertainment and communication, and unlock new possibilities for human experiences and interactions in the digital realm.

Virtual reality in augmented reality ecosystems

Virtual reality (VR) and augmented reality (AR) are two complementary technologies that are often discussed together due to their overlapping capabilities and potential for immersive experiences. While VR provides a fully simulated digital environment, AR overlays virtual elements onto the real world. The integration of VR within augmented reality ecosystems offers unique possibilities and benefits. Here are some key aspects of virtual reality in augmented reality ecosystems:

1. Enhanced Immersion: By combining VR and AR, users can experience a heightened level of immersion. Virtual reality can create fully immersive and interactive environments, while augmented reality enhances real-world surroundings with virtual overlays. This integration allows users to interact with both virtual and real elements simultaneously, creating a more immersive and engaging experience.

2. Seamless Transitions: Augmented reality ecosystems can seamlessly transition between VR and AR modes. Users can switch between fully virtual experiences and blended experiences that incorporate virtual objects into the real world. This flexibility enables diverse use cases, from immersive gaming to interactive educational content.

3. Contextual Interactions: Virtual reality in augmented reality ecosystems can leverage the real-world context to enhance user interactions. For example, virtual

objects can be placed and manipulated in real-world environments, allowing users to interact with them in a more intuitive and natural manner. This fusion of virtual and real elements opens up new possibilities for interactive storytelling, design visualization, and practical applications like interior decorating.

4. Mixed Reality Experiences: The combination of VR and AR can create mixed reality (MR) experiences, where virtual and real-world elements coexist and interact in real-time. MR blurs the line between the physical and digital realms, enabling compelling scenarios such as virtual objects reacting to real-world physics or virtual characters interacting with physical objects.

5. Collaboration and Social Interaction: Virtual reality within augmented reality ecosystems can facilitate collaborative and social experiences. Multiple users can share the same virtual environment while being physically present in the real world. This enables teamwork, communication, and shared experiences, whether it's working on a project, exploring a virtual museum together, or participating in multiplayer gaming.

6. Spatial Mapping and Object Recognition: Augmented reality ecosystems often employ spatial mapping and object recognition technologies to understand and interact with the real-world environment. These capabilities can be leveraged in VR experiences within AR ecosystems to enhance object interactions, enable realistic physics simulations, or align virtual content with real-world objects and surfaces.

7. Accessible AR Content Placement: Virtual reality can assist in the precise placement of AR content. By using VR to create and preview virtual objects and their positions, developers and content creators can ensure accurate and contextually appropriate placement within the real world. This approach helps streamline

the content creation process and ensures a seamless integration of virtual elements.

8. Extended Functionality and User Interfaces: Virtual reality can enhance the functionality and user interfaces of augmented reality ecosystems. VR can provide more immersive and interactive controls, such as gesture-based interactions or virtual hand tracking, which can be leveraged in AR applications. This combination allows for more intuitive and immersive user experiences.

The integration of virtual reality within augmented reality ecosystems offers a rich and diverse range of possibilities. The combined technologies provide a spectrum of experiences, from fully virtual simulations to blended interactions with the real world. This integration enhances immersion, promotes collaboration, and opens up new avenues for creativity, education, entertainment, and practical applications across various industries.

Virtual reality and artificial intelligence

Virtual reality (VR) and artificial intelligence (AI) are two transformative technologies that, when combined, have the potential to revolutionize various industries and reshape the way we interact with digital environments. Here are some key points about the relationship between virtual reality and artificial intelligence:

1. Enhanced Immersion: Artificial intelligence can enhance the immersion in virtual reality experiences by creating intelligent and responsive virtual characters and objects. AI algorithms can imbue virtual entities with realistic behaviors, emotions, and interactions, making the virtual environment feel more lifelike and engaging.

2. Intelligent Agents and NPCs: Virtual reality environments can be populated with intelligent agents or non-player characters (NPCs) powered by AI. These AI-driven entities can serve as guides, companions, opponents, or collaborators, adding depth and realism to virtual reality experiences. AI enables NPCs to exhibit human-like behaviors, adapt to user interactions, and provide dynamic and personalized experiences.

3. Adaptive and Personalized Experiences: AI algorithms can analyze user behavior and preferences in virtual reality and dynamically adjust the content and experience to suit individual needs. By leveraging machine learning and data analysis techniques, AI can deliver personalized recommendations, optimize virtual environments based on user preferences, and

create adaptive narratives tailored to each user's interactions.

4. Natural Language Processing and Voice Recognition: AI-powered natural language processing (NLP) and voice recognition technologies can enable users to interact with virtual reality environments using voice commands and engage in natural language conversations with virtual characters. This enhances the realism of interactions and allows for more intuitive and immersive experiences.

5. Intelligent Content Creation: AI can assist in the creation of virtual reality content by automating and enhancing various aspects of the design process. For example, AI algorithms can generate realistic landscapes, populate virtual worlds with objects and characters, or even dynamically generate content based on user preferences or real-time data inputs. This streamlines the content creation pipeline and enables the rapid development of immersive virtual reality experiences.

6. Data Analysis and Insights: Virtual reality environments generate vast amounts of data about user behavior, interactions, and preferences. AI can analyze this data to derive valuable insights, such as user engagement patterns, preferences for certain types of content, or areas for improvement in the virtual experience. These insights can inform the design of future virtual reality applications and help developers optimize the user experience.

7. AI-based Predictive Analytics: AI algorithms can leverage the data collected from virtual reality interactions to make predictions and recommendations. For example, AI can analyze user behavior and predict user preferences, allowing for personalized content recommendations or adaptive game mechanics. This helps create more engaging and

tailored virtual reality experiences.

8. Real-time Simulation and Adaptive Environments: AI algorithms can facilitate real-time simulation and adaptation of virtual reality environments. By continuously analyzing user inputs, AI can dynamically adjust the virtual environment, change the behavior of virtual entities, or modify the simulation parameters to create a more responsive and interactive experience.

The combination of virtual reality and artificial intelligence holds immense potential for enhancing user experiences, enabling intelligent interactions, and creating highly immersive and personalized virtual environments. The integration of AI technologies within virtual reality opens up new possibilities for entertainment, education, training, therapy, and many other domains where realistic simulations and intelligent interactions are desired. As both VR and AI continue to advance, their synergy will unlock exciting opportunities for innovation and transformative experiences.

Predictions for the future of virtual reality

The future of virtual reality (VR) is promising, and several trends and predictions can be made regarding its development and impact. Here are some key predictions for the future of virtual reality:

1. Enhanced Immersion: As technology continues to advance, VR experiences will become even more immersive, blurring the line between the physical and virtual worlds. Higher-resolution displays, improved graphics rendering, haptic feedback systems, and advanced motion tracking will contribute to a more realistic and engaging VR experience.

2. Expanded Applications: VR will find applications beyond gaming and entertainment. Industries such as education, healthcare, architecture, engineering, training, and remote collaboration will increasingly adopt VR for immersive simulations, virtual classrooms, medical procedures, architectural visualization, and virtual meetings, among other purposes. VR will revolutionize how we learn, work, and interact.

3. Wireless and Mobile VR: Wireless VR headsets and advancements in mobile computing power will make VR more accessible and portable. Standalone headsets and mobile devices with VR capabilities will enable users to experience VR without the need for tethered connections or high-end PCs, making VR more convenient and accessible to a broader audience.

4. Social VR and Shared Experiences: Virtual reality

will become more social, allowing users to interact and engage with others in virtual spaces. Social VR platforms will enable people to meet, communicate, collaborate, and share experiences in immersive virtual environments. This will facilitate virtual social gatherings, virtual classrooms, and virtual events, bringing people together regardless of geographical distances.

5. Augmented Reality (AR) Integration: Virtual reality and augmented reality will increasingly converge, leading to mixed reality experiences. Combining VR and AR technologies will enable users to seamlessly blend digital content with the real world, creating interactive and immersive experiences that integrate virtual objects and information into the user's physical environment.

6. Neural Interfaces and Brain-Computer Interfaces: Advancements in neural interfaces and brain-computer interfaces (BCIs) will enable direct interaction with virtual environments using brain signals. This technology may allow users to control virtual objects, navigate VR spaces, and experience virtual sensations directly through their thoughts, enhancing the immersion and interactivity of VR experiences.

7. Cloud-based VR: Cloud computing will play a significant role in the future of VR. Cloud-based VR platforms will leverage the computational power of remote servers to render complex graphics and deliver high-quality VR experiences to a wide range of devices, including low-end devices with limited processing capabilities.

8. AI Integration: Artificial intelligence (AI) will enhance VR experiences by creating more intelligent and realistic virtual entities, optimizing content generation and adaptation, and personalizing user experiences. AI algorithms will enable more natural and dynamic interactions within virtual environments, enhancing

immersion and user engagement.

9. Real-world Mapping and Digital Twins: VR will integrate with real-world mapping technologies and digital twin concepts, allowing users to explore virtual replicas of real-world locations and objects. This will have applications in areas such as urban planning, historical preservation, and virtual tourism, where users can virtually visit and interact with accurate representations of real-world places and artifacts.

10. Accessibility and Inclusivity: Efforts will continue to make VR more accessible and inclusive, addressing challenges such as motion sickness, physical limitations, and diverse user needs. Innovations in user interface design, input methods, and assistive technologies will enable a broader range of individuals to engage with and benefit from VR experiences.

These predictions highlight the immense potential of virtual reality to transform various aspects of our lives. While the future of VR is dynamic and ever-evolving, it is clear that VR will continue to advance, providing exciting and transformative experiences that reshape how we interact with digital content, environments, and each other.

Recap of key concepts and insights

Throughout this exploration of virtual reality (VR), we have covered a range of key concepts and insights. Here's a recap of some of the main points:

1. Definition and Concept: Virtual reality refers to a computer-generated simulation of a three-dimensional environment that can be interacted with and explored by an individual, creating a sense of presence and immersion.

2. Evolution and Significance: VR has evolved over several decades, starting from early experiments to the current state of advanced technology. Its potential impact spans various industries, including gaming, entertainment, education, healthcare, architecture, and more.

3. Immersive Experiences: VR offers unparalleled immersion by stimulating multiple senses, including visual, auditory, and in some cases, haptic feedback. The goal is to create a sense of presence, transporting users to virtual worlds and enabling them to interact with digital content.

4. Hardware Components: VR hardware includes headsets, controllers, and tracking systems. Headsets provide the visual and auditory experience, while controllers and tracking systems enable users to interact and navigate within the virtual environment.

5. Content Creation and Development: Creating VR content involves various tools and techniques such as 3D modeling, animation, and interactive storytelling. Content developers use specialized software and

platforms to design and build virtual environments.

6. Applications of VR: VR has found applications in gaming and entertainment, training and simulation, education, healthcare, architecture, travel and tourism, social interactions, and more. It enables immersive experiences, realistic simulations, and virtual collaborations in these domains.

7. Challenges and Considerations: VR faces challenges such as hardware limitations, user comfort and health concerns, content accessibility, ethical considerations, privacy issues, and legal and regulatory aspects. Overcoming these challenges requires continuous innovation, research, and responsible development.

8. Future Trends: The future of VR holds several exciting possibilities. Predictions include enhanced immersion, expanded applications beyond gaming, wireless and mobile VR, social interactions in virtual spaces, integration with augmented reality, advancements in AI and neural interfaces, and cloud-based VR experiences.

9. Impact and Transformation: VR has the potential to transform how we learn, work, communicate, entertain, and experience the world around us. It opens up new avenues for creativity, collaboration, and exploration, empowering individuals and industries alike.

10. Accessibility and Inclusivity: Ensuring VR is accessible to all individuals, regardless of physical abilities or other limitations, is crucial. Efforts to improve user experience, address motion sickness, and incorporate assistive technologies are essential for fostering inclusivity.

In summary, virtual reality represents a groundbreaking technology that enables immersive experiences and opens up endless possibilities across various fields. Its evolution and impact continue to shape the way we interact with digital content, environments, and each other. The future of VR holds great promise, and it will undoubtedly play a significant role in transforming our lives in the years to come.

Inspiring readers to embrace virtual reality

As we conclude this exploration of virtual reality (VR), it is essential to inspire readers to embrace this transformative technology. Here are some key points to encourage individuals to dive into the world of VR:

1. Limitless Possibilities: Virtual reality unlocks a realm of boundless possibilities. By immersing yourself in virtual environments, you can experience things that were once unimaginable. From exploring fantastical worlds to stepping into historical moments, VR offers a level of engagement and immersion that surpasses traditional media.

2. Empowering Experiences: VR empowers you to take control of your digital adventures. Whether it's gaming, education, or creative expression, VR puts you at the center of the action, allowing you to shape your own experiences and narratives. The power to create, learn, and explore in ways you've never imagined is within your reach.

3. Enhancing Real-World Connections: Virtual reality doesn't replace the real world; it enhances it. VR offers new avenues for connection, collaboration, and communication. Engage in social experiences, collaborate with others remotely, or attend virtual events and conferences, all while breaking the barriers of physical distance.

4. Personal Growth and Learning: VR is a gateway to personal growth and expanded learning opportunities. Dive into educational simulations, acquire new skills

through immersive training programs, or embark on virtual travel experiences that broaden your horizons. The potential for self-improvement and knowledge acquisition in VR is immense.

5. Unleashing Creativity: Virtual reality unleashes your creativity by providing tools and platforms to express yourself in immersive ways. Design virtual worlds, create stunning artworks, develop interactive experiences, and bring your imagination to life. VR offers a canvas where your ideas can take shape and captivate others.

6. Transforming Industries: VR is reshaping industries, from entertainment and gaming to healthcare, education, and beyond. By embracing VR, you become a part of this transformative wave, contributing to its evolution and making an impact in your field of interest.

7. Community and Collaboration: VR fosters vibrant communities of like-minded enthusiasts, creators, and professionals. By joining these communities, you gain access to a wealth of knowledge, inspiration, and collaboration opportunities. Share your passion, learn from others, and contribute to the collective growth of the VR ecosystem.

8. Embracing the Future: Virtual reality is not a passing trend; it's a technological revolution that is here to stay. By embracing VR, you position yourself at the forefront of innovation and future possibilities. Don't miss out on being a part of this exciting era of digital transformation.

So, let go of any hesitation and embrace virtual reality. Dive into the immersive experiences, connect with others in new ways, unleash your creativity, and explore the limitless frontiers of the virtual realm. The future of VR is waiting for you, and by embracing it, you can shape your own extraordinary journey.

Final thoughts on the transformative power of virtual reality

In conclusion, virtual reality (VR) possesses transformative power that extends far beyond its technological advancements. It has the potential to revolutionize how we experience, interact, and perceive the world around us. Through the immersive nature of VR, we can transcend physical limitations, unlock new realms of creativity, and forge connections that bridge distances.

VR enables us to step into new dimensions, whether they are fantastical worlds, educational simulations, or professional training environments. It empowers us to redefine storytelling, gaming, entertainment, and various industries. By blurring the boundaries between the digital and physical realms, VR has the capacity to reshape our perceptions, expand our knowledge, and deepen our empathy.

Furthermore, virtual reality has the remarkable ability to bring people together, fostering communities and collaboration on a global scale. It transcends geographical barriers, enabling us to connect, communicate, and share experiences with others in ways previously unimaginable. The sense of presence and shared immersion in VR can cultivate deeper connections and facilitate meaningful interactions.

However, the transformative power of VR also comes with responsibility. We must navigate the ethical considerations, privacy concerns, and societal impacts that arise with the widespread adoption of this technology. It is essential to ensure inclusivity, accessibility, and user well-being, while also addressing challenges such as motion sickness, hardware limitations, and content diversity.

As VR continues to evolve and become more accessible, it is crucial for individuals, industries, and policymakers to embrace its potential and actively contribute to its growth. By exploring the possibilities, pushing boundaries, and fostering innovation, we can shape the future of VR and harness its transformative power for the betterment of society.

In this ever-expanding virtual landscape, let us embrace the transformative power of virtual reality and embark on a journey of exploration, creativity, collaboration, and personal growth. Together, we can unlock the full potential of VR and create a future where the boundaries of the physical and digital worlds seamlessly merge, offering us infinite possibilities and transformative experiences.

www.ingramcontent.com/pod-product-compliance
Lightning Source LLC
LaVergne TN
LVHW022125060326
832903LV00063B/4072